GETTING ALONG
WITH PEOPLE
WHO DON'T GET ALONG

Dianna Daniels Booher

BROADMAN PRESS
Nashville, Tennessee

© Copyright 1984 • Broadman Press
All rights reserved.

4252-09
ISBN: 0-8054-5209-5

Dewey Decimal Classification: 158
Subject Heading: Human relations

Library of Congress Catalog Card Number: 83-14406

Printed in the United States of America

Library of Congress Cataloging in Publication Data

Booher, Dianna Daniels.
  Getting along with people who don't get along.

  1. Interpersonal relations—Biblical teaching.
2. Interpersonal communication—Biblical teaching.
I. Title.
HM132.B66 1984   302.3'4   83-14406
ISBN 0-8054-5209-5

To
Members of
Metropolitan Baptist Church

Contents

Introduction

Although I've not completed a formal scientific survey, my theory is that more people leave churches as the result of interpersonal conflicts than because of theological differences.

And this same interpersonal ineptness spills over into discontent in secular jobs as well as in families. Engineers resign lucrative jobs because they can't work effectively with project team members, not because they can't design a building to meet a client's need; secretaries transfer from boss to boss, trying to find one who praises rather than disparages their letter-editing skills; teachers leave the classroom still enamored with teaching but tired of departmental politics. In fact, a comprehensive survey of 1,200 middle-level supervisors revealed that as little as 13 percent of their total job success related to technical skill. Fully 87 percent of their success stemmed from their ability to get along with other people.[1]

Likewise, marriage counselors reveal that few marriages break up over major differences in values and goals. More marriages break up over conflict in expressing and receiving love. Not over how much money to spend on the relatives' Christmas gifts, but that more was spent on one set of in-laws than the other. Not over a change in occupations, but over lack of communication about the division of household responsibilities. Not over disciplining a child, but over whether that discipline should be achieved through praise of acceptable behavior or criticism of the unacceptable.

In other words, people have trouble with the *how* rather than the *what* of living, working, and worshiping with others.

But interpersonal conflict among Christians isn't a twentieth-century problem. Old Testament Daniel had his share of conflicts with kings, and he had to devise creative alternatives in problem solving, while still showing respect to those in authority. Martha and Mary, as well as Abraham and Lot, let family disputes interfere with God's best for them. Arguments and jealousy broke out among the disciples as they vied among themselves for positions of greatest importance. Barnabas and Paul, though both devoted to the cause of evangelism, found it expedient to part company due to their disagreement about travel itinerary and companions. The Greek and Hebrew widows turned the New Testament church on its ear with a dispute over who was receiving the most attention and food from the church community. On a larger scale, the first-century Christians found it necessary to call a Jerusalem Council to formulate guidelines to quiet the conflict over Jewish laws and customs. Confrontation was no foreign element to Jesus Christ himself, when challenged by unbelievers in the crowds and money changers in the Temple.

Although, of course, all relationships do not necessarily center around conflict, they grow as a result of effective communication skills in the areas of advice, criticism, forgiveness, and peacemaking. For example, the simple act of asking for advice is not such a simple act after all. Recall the trouble King Rehoboam had, when he chose to seek advice from his close friends (rather than the wiser, older leaders) about how to treat his kingdom subjects? On the other hand, you will also remember the positive results of the advice given by Paul when he suggested that runaway slave Onesimus return to his master Philemon.

Modern-day church squabbles over what color to paint the preschool area or whether a deacon should hold the position of treasurer tell us that we still have not mastered the biblical principles of effective communication and conflict resolution. Glibly quoted platitudes and principles need practical translation.

What does loving someone really mean? That you will never criticize an attitude or behavior? That you can have unjustified criticism leveled at you by a fellow Christian without developing resentment? That you will always give the advice another wants to hear? That you always accept the advice someone offers who claims to be advising under the leadership of the Holy Spirit? That you will go along with a committee decision that you believe to be a poor one? That you swallow hard to keep quiet when someone offends you? That you insist that two quarreling friends forget their differences and keep the peace at all cost?

Because Christianity is not a philosophy but a relationship with Jesus Christ, we practice our faith by establishing relationships and dealing with others by his example. This book attempts to give help in this oft-neglected, sometimes generalized, area of practical application of faith—people skills at church, work, or home.

1

"We just have a personality clash."

Chiseling the Jagged Edges Off Your Personality

A schoolteacher and a lawyer sit on opposite sides of the church auditorium each Sunday. When they meet in neutral territory, they merely nod, flash a plastic smile, and pass without words. Both are careful to ask for the names of other committee members before they agree to serve. By mutual agreement, they have a "personality clash" and try to stay out of each other's way as much as possible.

But wait a minute. Are Christians entitled to have "personality clashes" with their fellowmen? That is not to say that people don't have *differences* in temperament and behavioral makeup. On the contrary: One person who moves in the fast lane gets assignments done yesterday; another contemplates the best method for weeks before moving into action. Some of us speak about four hundred words a minute with gusts up to six hundred; others drag out their thoughts so that it is the epitome of restraint not to finish sentences for them! But should these two persons allow their different mind-sets and behaviors to create a barrier between them?

Some people have "written off" half the church, their families, the neighborhood, or the work place due to such "personality clashes." When Paul wrote of Christians as different parts of the body of Christ—eyes, ears, nose, and throat—his metaphor described a context of unity, not dissension. Perhaps the cry "personality clash" has become the escape hatch of the century for many Christians who have negligible people skills, unforgiving spirits, and offensive behavior and words.

If you yourself seem to be clashing with more and more people (or they seem to be clashing with you), perhaps it's time to do a little self-examination to see if you might have serious people problems which need correcting. Below is a checklist to help you determine if improvements are in order.

1. Do you regret conversations, wishing you'd said things differently or not at all?

2. When you speak, do you feel that people really don't pay attention to what you say?

3. Do others try to "interpret" for you and add to your comments?

4. Do people seem to avoid sharing information with you or to avoid coming to you with personal concerns, seldom asking for advice or a listening ear?

5. When two mutual friends get upset with each other, do you try to "stay out of it"?

6. When you ask for advice, do you feel that the advice often is not really usable?

7. When you look at others' behavior, do you notice what they are doing wrong more often than what they are doing right?

8. Do you feel unduly criticized and get blamed for things you had no part in?

9. Do you feel defensive when someone discusses a problem or conflict with you?

10. Do people "get their feelings hurt" by things you say?

11. Do your conversations often turn into what others call "arguments"?

12. Do you lose your temper with people?

13. Do you ever "brood" over things people say to you, turning the comments over and over in your mind, trying to decide exactly what they mean?

14. Do you just "let conflicts ride" because it's easier than discussing them with the other person?

15. Do you wish people wouldn't bother you with their personal problems?

16. Does your mind wander when others are talking to you, and do you find yourself faking attention?

17. Do you feel uncomfortable making or accepting apologies?

Have the questions scratched enough surfaces so that you have some idea of the extent of your rough edges and interpersonal conflicts? If so, the place to start filing off these jagged protrusions is with yourself and your own perceptions. Let me illustrate:

During intermission at a seminar, a group of people you know are talking and laughing together in the hallway. Because you introduced the morning's speaker to the seminar audience and have been sitting on the platform, you have not had a chance to speak individually to the people you know. As you watch the hallway group talking and laughing, you may have one of several perceptions: (1) They are discussing events and topics completely unrelated to the seminar—a good restaurant for lunch or the morning traffic. (2) They are discussing how informative the seminar is and how appropriate your introduction was. (3) They consider the seminar a waste of time so far and are making fun of your introduction and the speaker.

The third reaction, of course, is typical of someone who has self-doubt and projects that low esteem onto others with no provocation whatsoever. Many people who feel conflicts with others merely have to change the way they "talk" to themselves, and others' imaginary poor treatment of them will vanish.

If only it could be that easy for everybody!

Changing that self-doubt to self-confidence centers around the belief that God made you and loves you just because you're you. By believing that with your emotions, as well as with your mind, you can eliminate many of the "conflicts" you see others initiating toward you. Instead, you are free to work on real barriers that your own attitudes or actions may have erected. In other words, you are free to work on the rough edges.

Rough Edges

Hostility

Few Christians engage in fist fights. Even our secular relationships have a more civilized appearance, and much is hidden behind a blank or angry stare, or even a smug smile. Even when someone calls another's hand on bad feelings and asks if the person is upset or offended about something, the answer is generally: "No, of course not. Whatever made you think so?"

As a result, we may begin to doubt our own ability to "read" a situation and determine someone's true attitude. Nevertheless, most clues are accurate, no matter the denials.

If you are one to "cover" your feelings and you seldom tell others when they have hurt you, perhaps you have been misled into thinking that your own hostility doesn't show. But a hostile attitude usually does "show," and it creates further problems. Our own bodies react to show this emotional upset through yawning, glazed eyes, foot or finger tapping, rigid posture, rapid heartbeat, clenched fists, tensing of facial muscles, reddening. And not only do our bodies betray us but our words and actions, no matter how guarded, often fail to disguise our hostility.

Of course, we recognize blunt belligerence in conversations, wrapped in words, phrases, or statements similar to the following: "certainly," "undoubtedly," "you're wrong," "you don't know what you're talking about." But more subtle forms of hostility seep into conversations through such habits as always "topping" someone else's story, accomplishments, or good luck with a tale of your own; shooting down others' ideas almost before they have a chance to express them; or pointedly questioning everything someone does— as if doubting their motives, expertise, or both.

Hostility is hard to hide. If you feel it, you probably reveal it.

Defensiveness

When around a defensive person, you often feel as if your conversations are short-circuiting somewhere, but it's difficult to locate the exact problem. Your encounters move along these lines:

"Do you know where that yellow note pad is?"
"I haven't had it."

"The speaker for the board doesn't seem too knowledgeable."
"Well, it wasn't my idea to invite her."

"Every year our committee seems to reinvent the wheel; we need to elect members to serve for longer terms and to adopt a rotation system, don't you think?"

"Well, I'll be glad to resign my seat; I didn't ask for the job."

If you find yourself frequently reacting from a defensive mode, learn to recognize and freeze that behavior. It constantly forces others onto eggshells, lest they "hurt your feelings."

If there's one person in particular who makes you defensive, try to figure out what about that person pushes your hurt button. Is there fear that he or she does not hold high something you consider sacred? Perhaps what the person says or does makes you feel diminished in some way. Or you may simply be insulted to think that "reason" cannot win out in a certain situation. If you can understand why you have an adverse reaction to someone, you will have gone a long way in learning more about yourself.

For example, in the dialogue about the committee, consider what would make a person feel threatened enough to respond as she did. Does she feel incapable of serving on the committee? Does she feel that the others' work will show hers to be inferior? Does she feel that the others don't really want to work with her? Whatever triggers this defensiveness, it usually shows up in a barbed-wire protective attitude that scratches and nicks people as they approach your sensitive spots.

Competitiveness/Rivalry

We all compete says Harvey L. Ruben in his book *Competing, Understanding, and Winning the Strategic Games We All Play.* Even the person who says he is not competitive really means that he is not competitive overtly. In one sense, we competed even in our mother's womb for food and exercise. And, happily or unhappily, we have practiced competition in family, school, sports, and business ever since.[1]

Other researchers have distinguished between competition and rivalry. Terry Orlick says that competition is seeking to gain what someone else is seeking to gain at the same time. Rivalry, on the other hand, is behavior directed against another person, while the object or position for which they compete is only secondary.[2] We see this distinction daily among children in a family; "the biggest piece of pie" or "sitting in the bean-bag chair" has little to do with eating or resting. Instead, each request is an attempt to put the other down in the eyes of the parent and to ensure himself of more love.

Usually, in fact, the closer the relationship or the more equally skilled two people are, the more intense their rivalry. People seldom have hard feelings toward someone who is markedly superior to them. Amateur golfers rarely feel competitive toward Arnold Palmer, but they do envy a brother-in-law who consistently shoots two strokes under them. Or the salesperson who outsells you by only two hundred dollars creates more intense stress than the vice-president of the company, who outsells you by thousands.

Check it out in your own experience. Are you really competing *for* a particular goal, or do you feel rivalry *against* someone, while the goal is secondary? If your situation is one of rivalry, find out why: How does this person's winning diminish you? How does winning make you feel superior? Why is your self-worth tied to this one prize, position, honor?

Joe Girard, who is in the *Guinness Book of World Records* for selling the most cars in one year, tells of his experience when his company honored him for his achievements. The first year in which he sold the most cars, his peers cheered at the big banquet and celebration in his honor. The second year when he outsold everyone, the applause among his peers was noticeably subdued. At the third annual recognition banquet for the same feat, his wife cried as the crowd booed his good fortune.[3]

Anxiety, stress, and hurt feelings often crop up in situations where there can be only one winner. This was the case when the mother of James and John asked Jesus for the two most prestigious seats of honor for her sons when Jesus came into his kingdom. Immediately, the other disciples began to grumble over a potential loss which they had hitherto not even contemplated. Had he granted the request and given away the "best two seats in the kingdom," no doubt rivalry would have continued among them. But once Jesus explained the real nature of his kingdom and greatness—to be of service rather than to be served—we have no further record of the disciples vying for position around him. You see, Jesus had many "prizes" or places of service to offer.

Unfortunately, rivalry and jealousy are still apparent among God's twentieth-century followers. Pastors snipe at one another more often from a rivalry about the size of their respective congregations than about theological differences. Bible study teachers feel cheated if more new members are added to the rolls of another's class than to their own. Teens compete over who gets the best solo in the musical and refuse to participate at all if another gets the role. Many Christians have no trouble at all weeping with another person over his burdens, but many have difficulty in taking Paul's advice of Romans 12:15 to rejoice with another's good fortune.

To stop this sense of rivalry, find ways to make yourself feel more confident without downgrading another. And when you see evidence of another's jealousy toward you, you can lessen the rivalry by making an effort to build the other's self-esteem. Show honest admiration for his skill, position, or accomplishments. Humble yourself to ask for his advice or help. Finally, attempt to create more "prizes" and more opportunities for both of you to succeed.

Aloofness

Eric Berne's work in the area of transactional analysis brought us words and phrases like "strokes," "warm fuzzies," and "cold pricklies" to describe our verbal responses to each other. We came to recognize the universal need for those verbal and behavioral pats on the back that mean we are OK people, noticed and appreciated.

The apostle Paul certainly knew the value of strokes. Instead of holding himself up as that "great itinerant preacher hero," he shared the glory, specifically mentioning his helpers in his letters and pointing out their contributions to the faith and his own comfort. If you haven't evaluated your stroke style lately, perhaps you alienate people simply through neglecting to acknowledge their presence or significance. What you consider shy or reserved behavior, others around you may take as aloofness or disdain. People with a selfish stroke style rarely say hello, engage in small talk, smile, tease, laugh, or compliment another on achievement.

Practice meeting others' needs in these small ways that pay big dividends in opening the way to better relationships.

Blowing Your Own Horn

In the business world, accomplishments often go unrecognized and unrewarded unless they are documented in a memo for the next higher-up to notice. It is difficult to shift to a lower gear in dealing with peers outside the work arena.

Robert Weiss, an educator and psychiatrist, has delineated four types of relationships that people must have to make them feel happy and well adjusted. One of these types is a relationship with people who respect our abilities. And when, through a move from church to church, community to community, or school to school, we "lost our audience," we feel a strong need to recapture that respect and reestablish our strengths. When no opportunities arise to "prove ourselves" or when recognition doesn't come soon enough, we are tempted to tell others of our accomplishments, so that they will show us the respect we need to keep our self-esteem intact.[4]

The problem is, most of us would rather be shown than told. Constant talk of personal accomplishments, possessions, or positions drives people away from us faster than a contagious disease. "Let another man praise thee, and not thine own mouth" (Prov. 27:2).

Gossip

The next time you find yourself sharing tidbits of information with someone, ask yourself who is doing most of the sharing and who is doing most of the listening. If you're a gossip, you probably already have a reputation that makes others hesitant to tell you anything personal that they don't want spread and hesitant to be seen with you for fear of guilt-by-association.

To stop yourself from this bad habit, analyze why you feel the compulsion to talk about others' lives and problems. Is idleness the reason? If so, find something constructive to occupy your time. Do you feel important by sharing "news" that others don't have? Do you think giving "inside information" wins friends? If any of these is the case, recognize that your problem is lack of self-esteem and try to build your confidence in other, more appropriate ways.

Before you start to say something about someone else, try these screening questions: Will the subject of the "news" be helped by my telling this information? Could the person possibly be harmed? "The words of a talebearer are as wounds, and they go down into the innermost parts of the belly" (Prov. 26:22). Many who wouldn't dream of physically attacking another individual cut someone with their tongues and leave them for dead, without even giving the words a second thought. When in doubt, leave it out.

Prophesying Gloom and Doom

Some people look at a cloud-free blue sky, feel a refreshing breeze, enjoy soothing sunshine, and then complain, "Too bad it can't stay this way forever." The world holds enough worries for today without taking on those of tomorrow, as Jesus said in his Sermon on the Mount. "Sufficient unto the day is the evil thereof" (Matt. 6:34).

Just as cheerfulness is contagious, so is gloominess; others avoid prophets of gloom and doom out of a sense of self-protection from depression. You remember how many friends the prophet Elijah collected while sitting under the juniper tree, don't you?

But, you say, I have worked the jagged edges off my own personality; I don't feel hostile, defensive, jealous, aloof, or arrogant, nor do I prophesy doom and gloom. You've dealt with your own motives, interests, and insecurities, and feel as though you're finally on neutral ground in meeting others where they stand. Then you're ready to build an effective, supportive relationship with another person.

We're down to one last area of attention in eliminating "personality clashes"—take care to develop attractive traits, traits that magnetize and draw others.

Personality Positives

Cheerfulness

Practice smiling, nodding, and small talk with those you encounter. Given two grocery checkout lines of the same length, which one are you most likely to choose—the one where the checker smiles and wishes customers a good day or the one where the checker scowls and moans to the sacker that she's past due for a break?

"A merry heart doeth good like a medicine" (Prov. 17:22). Not only for you, but for the other person. Be someone's medicine. Cheerfulness attracts; grumpiness repels.

Tolerance

Tolerance means granting people the right to be different and squelching the urge to show them "the best way." It means agreeing to let someone disagree with you without having to go out of your way to prove him wrong. It means buying your daughter a lavender evening gown when you know she looks best in the green one. It means letting your colleague eat her lunch at the desk even though the smell of ham-on-rye bothers you. It even means letting your neighbor use his Sundays to honor God in whatever way he thinks appropriate. To eat meat offered to idols, to keep the Jewish holidays and customs—to each his own under God's leadership, Paul says in Romans 14.

Jesus, too, tolerated the weak faith of those who came to him, tolerated the limited understanding of his followers about his kingdom, tolerated their sometimes unorthodox way of serving him. When John complained to him that another was casting out devils but not following along with the disciples' group, Jesus responded: "Forbid him not: . . . For he that is not against us is on our part" (Mark 9:39).

Tolerance. Do you have the tolerance Jesus had, or are you ready to pull your sword as Peter did and lop off the ears of someone who doesn't believe or practice what you do?

Energy

For centuries, the old have said to the young, "I wish I had your energy." Yet we all know of people who become energyless long before they get old. A continual supply of creative energy comes from the living source Jesus spoke of when he said, "I have meat to eat that you know not of" (John 4:32). His divine mission gave him sustenance when other resources were lacking.

Cultivate yourself by reading, thinking, conversing, and meditating on God's Word so that you have energy to "give" when people come into contact with you. Be strong and ask for wisdom to help others grow and reach their potential. A friend of mine invited preacher and writer Ralph Neighbors and my family to her home for lunch after he'd spoken at our morning worship service. When, soon after lunch, Dr. Neighbors left, my hostess friend flopped in her chair exhausted. Expecting her to be relieved that the rush and noise were over, I was surprised at, but understood, her comment: "Isn't it fabulous having someone like him over? It's so much trouble, but you always get so much. I feel like a sponge."

An overriding purpose and daily goals provide you with the energy that electrifies your personality and even charges those who come into contact with you.

Empathy

Have you ever sat in an audience listening to a speech or sermon when the speaker lost his train of thought and became flustered? If your face began to redden with his and you began to feel sweaty palms and pray for his recovery, then you're acquainted with empathy.

On the other hand, you probably sensed from the squirming in the group or heard from the criticisms afterwards that not all onlookers reacted with such charity. Fortunately, when I give my business writing workshops before corporate clients, and occasionally lose my train of thought in mid-sentence, I catch the expression of those in the group and mentally divide them into two groups—

the merciful and the indifferent. It's the lifted eyebrow, the up-turned, encouraging smile that helps me to regain my composure.

Empathy is a tenderness that makes your heart melt even when the heat is turned on someone else.

Tact

You've heard many describe themselves with the following re-mark, "I'm just the sort of person who says what he thinks." What's more, they sound as if they're describing a virtue!

Do you think that when Jesus called tax collector Zacchaeus down from the tree, he started their relationship by pointing out that Zacchaeus cheated? I doubt it. I believe Jesus probably let his own goodness work its work in this man's heart until he became aware of what he needed to change.

Solomon spoke directly of tact when describing the virtuous woman of Proverbs 31:26b: "When she speaks, her words are wise, and kindness is the rule for everything she says" (TLB).

Most people are not intentionally rude; they're simply thought-less. Thinking something is no justification for saying it. Tact has an impact all its own.

Dependability

Dependability involves never giving way to the urge to cover by saying, "I'm sorry" or by making excuses. The man in Jesus' parable who hid his one talent for fear of losing it offered excuses. Dependability means accomplishment rather than excuse. Depend-ability means underscoring your intentions with actions.

A dependable worker who works "as unto the Lord" pays attention to the details of his job and carries out the intent and spirit of all assignments and directions, as well as the literal meaning of the command. Dependable means being steadfast, faithful, punc-tual, and thorough.

Helpfulness

In our day, when the Boy Scout's attempt to help a little old lady with an armful of packages across the street has become the stuff of slapstick comedy, helpfulness involves almost any act of caring. It means breaking your stride to give someone the time of day; it means cleaning someone's house when he or she is ill; it means providing information, even when someone's too shy to ask.

The writer of Ecclesiastes points out the results of such a helpful, cooperative attitude: "Two can accomplish more than twice as much as one, for the results can be much better. If one falls, the other pulls him up; but if a man falls when he is alone, he's in trouble" (Eccl. 4:9-10, TLB).

Although not simply referring to a physical fall, the passage brings to mind a letter to the editor published in the *Houston Chronicle*, showing that such helpfulness, though rare, still occurs. A Chicagoan fell and broke her arm while crossing a downtown street. Seeing the accident, a Houston woman came to her aid and called her own husband, who took off work, drove them to the hospital emergency room, and waited. At ten-thirty in the evening, when the doctor had finished setting the arm, the lady insisted that the visitor come to her home for the evening where she could attend to her if there were any complications. Then the next morning, the Houston woman drove the injured woman to the airport to catch her plane—not a minor act itself, considering morning rush-hour traffic in Houston.

Since such helpfulness is a rare thing in our day, the injured lady had written her thanks in an open letter to the editor. Helpfulness refreshes others' spirits—particularly in a society in which it's no longer expected.

Positive Mental Outlook

Positive thinking means knowing who you are—someone whom God loves. It means understanding and concentrating on your assets and values rather than on your liabilities and failures. It demands living in the present, with blinders blocking off the past. It means making a commitment to specific goals to develop your fullest potential.

Perhaps some people are born with a positive outlook. Writer Robert J. McKain credits such an attitude to World War II General

Creighton Abrams. When he and his men were totally surrounded by the enemy, Abrams responded, "Gentlemen, for the first time in the history of this campaign, we are now in a position to attack the enemy in any direction."[5]

For those of you who don't come by positive thinking naturally, take a lesson from Paul. He kept a positive outlook about the future, even from a prison cell: (1) He stayed in tune with God. (2) He kept himself surrounded with loving friends, who offered encouragement. (3) He stayed busy—writing letters, sharing his faith, settling disputes between runaway slaves and masters, praying for the churches he'd established, organizing the work around him. (4) He fed his mind; one of the last favors he asked Timothy was to bring his books, especially the parchments or Scriptures. (5) He always had a goal—pressing on toward the mark of his high calling. Specifically, that meant daily, weekly, monthly plans, to travel wherever God sent him—even to Spain where no work had yet begun. If you can't be as positive as Paul, at least be pragmatic. Do what you can to change a bad situation; forget the rest.

Shaping your personality into a smooth, priceless diamond is definitely a task for a lifetime. But with Jesus as stonecutter, progress is steady and sure.

2

"He didn't hear a word I said" or "What you say is what you get"

Communication Capers

Check yourself the next time you wander into a book store and pick up a novel. Chances are that if you open the novel and skim through it, the parts you'll read will be bits and snatches of dialogue, not the long narrative passages. Why? Because most scenes that move the story along involve dialogue. Dialogue is at the heart of all relationships, whether the characters are in love or in conflict.

So it is with for-real people. Communication is what moves our relationships forward or backward. People don't make friends, make enemies, make a living, or make a marriage without the effort involved in talking and listening to others. Yet for all its importance, communication doesn't get much "formal" attention, other than English classes in school—in which 90 percent of the effort is directed toward studying the written language, an altogether different proposition.

Perhaps the neglect is due to the fact that everybody talks, and so we assume that communication comes as naturally as breathing. It's not until we get communication hiccups that we decide to pay a little attention to the specifics. Straightening out some of the communication capers is infinitely more complicated than holding your breath and taking ten swallows of water.

Communication is a two-way street, a shared experience, no matter how much skill you have developed in communicating. Your effectiveness, therefore, is diminished to some extent by the other person's ineptness.

In other words, communication involves several steps: your forming the thought, turning the thought into words, saying the words aloud with the proper verbal and nonverbal signals—and the other person's receiving the words, decoding them into meaning, and finally feeding back an appropriate response to show that the original thought was received. Communication is a fifty-fifty proposition, when it's done well. That means if the other person is a poor communicator, you have to make up the difference in effort in order to understand each other. Communication with some people may be a fifty-fifty effort, while with others, it's a ninety-ten task on your part.

After talking to a ninety-ten communicator, you often think to yourself: "He didn't hear a word I said," or "What you say is what you get." Someone hears your words with his ears but fails to apply his mind. A husband hears you say that you're too tired to cook dinner, but he doesn't understand your plea for help or your request for sympathy because of a rough day. As a result, you get what you said: "Oh, so you're not cooking dinner tonight? What are we supposed to do for something to eat?"

Psychologists have been busy for years describing the communication phenomenon in hopes that once we all understand where the other person is coming from, perhaps we can meet him half-way. Probably the most recently famous communication specialists are Eric Berne and Thomas A. Harris.

Berne, in his best-seller *Games People Play*, says that we all "transact" (communicate with others) from one of three ego states: parent, adult, child. A "normal" person operates from all three states from time to time, but primarily functions from his "adult." The parent "tape" represents what we heard as a child from our parents and produces comments and responses that protect, support, correct, rule, or judge others. The "adult" tape represents our reasoning abilities and our efforts to seek and send factual information among persons of equal status. The child "tape" reflects our childhood experiences and perceptions and produces comments that show rebellion, creativity, innocence, excitement, or selfishness—all traits of childhood.

For example, in a church board meeting, you may hear "transactions" from one person as he moves from ego states during the course of the meeting:

PARENT: "I told them that we shouldn't have hired that man as custodian; he seems shiftless."

ADULT: "I recommend that we appoint a committee to talk to the custodian about our dissatisfaction before we vote to fire him."

CHILD: "I like him, and if he gets fired, then maybe I should just resign, too."

The idea is to keep the "adult" in control the majority of the time, so that we can deal positively with the "adult" in other people.

Psychologist Thomas Harris suggests that persons are dominated by four life positions: I'm not OK—You're OK; I'm not OK—You're not OK; I'm OK—You're not OK; and I'm OK—You're OK. Of course, the desirable mind-set from which to communicate with other people is the last.[1]

Though these theories go far in helping us understand our own and others' motivations and reactions, most of us need more help with what goes in between—the ABC's of sending and receiving accurate messages.

What we say is one of the easier behavioral changes to make. Have tongue, can control. Therefore, the remainder of this chapter is outlined in such a way as to help you flip through your mind's file and figure out what has gone wrong in various conversational capers. The suggestions should help you make improvements in technique and to communicate in a positive, honest, and supportive manner.

A—Accepting Attitude

To keep communication lines open beyond the perfunctory comments, we must have an accepting attitude, one that shows respect and support for another's feelings and behavior even when we don't agree. It's much like the attitude we have about First Amendment rights—I may not agree with what you say, but I believe in your right to say it.

That does not mean we can't work to influence or change those ideas or feelings but rather that we don't try to shut them up inside. Some people are unaware of the effect they have on others with their, "oh, really," "that's interesting," "how nice," and "hmmmm" responses to what others share. In order for people to communicate with us, we must accept what they say, when they say it, for what it's worth—to them, not us. And what it's worth to them is encouragement to keep on trying to communicate.

B—Bloopers

Brace yourself; communication bloopers are bound to happen. And when they do, life will go on. Have you ever found yourself in a situation similar to one of the following?

● "We were talking about spring suit sales, and I mentioned a couple of stores where I had shopped the previous Saturday. After saying that I had chosen a conservatively tailored suit, I went into a detailed description of one I thought particularly outlandish. A lady standing in the circle with me sheepishly spoke up, 'That's what I bought yesterday.'"

● "We were talking about being afraid to be out on the streets alone at night because of the violence. Then I said something about having to drive through a particularly rough neighborhood. Later I found out that the person I was talking to lived in that neighborhood."

● "After a conference that I had been asked to lead for the first time, several of the attendees had come up to the front to talk to me afterward. One of the men shook my hand and said, 'You know, I've been coming to these conferences for years and never got a thing out of them. I came for purely social reasons. The instructor never gave us much. But for the first time, I'm really going home with a lot of information and I thank you.' Known to everyone in the circle, but the speaker, stood the brother of the man who had instructed the conference for the last few years."

Bloopers like this, yours and others', certainly can be the basis for hard feelings if not handled properly. But since no one is goof proof, try to handle your own mistakes with either humor or a sincere apology.

If it's not a serious blooper, you may try something like, "I'm known in this part of the country for my quick tongue and slow mind." Or, if the goof is something more offensive, give an honest apology: "That was a thoughtless statement and, in fact, shows my

ignorance. Will you please forgive me?" Most people are generous
with forgiveness when your intentions weren't to hurt and when
the apology is sincere.

When someone else blunders at your expense, she will be
eternally grateful if you will take the initiative in putting her at ease.
Again humor is appropriate: "That's OK. I can play deaf on demand."
Or, "Score one; the next insult's on me." Be sure to smile genuinely
so that the other person knows you hold no grudge and have not
attributed the blunder to intentional injury.

In dealing with a few people who make a goof at your expense, the
ball will be entirely in your court to be gracious. Being unsure of
themselves and defensive, they may expect, and even read into
future situations, your attempt to "get even." That's when you'll have
to go 90 percent of the way to keep a cordial relationship and show
them that you're not keeping score.

C—Call Names

In Romans 16, Paul called the names of twenty-six people in his
greetings. Did you ever wonder why he didn't just say, "Tell
everybody hello"? Individuals were important to him. Can you
imagine what kind of memory he must have had to remember all the
believers in town after town where he traveled? And can you see the
pleasure on various faces when his letters were read before the
group and people heard their names called as Paul's special friends?

A person's name is music to his ears. If you don't believe it, see
how fast he corrects you when you mispronounce it. When you can't
even remember it, you certainly erect a communication barrier. Pay
particular attention when entering a group; calling everyone's name
at least once during the conversation lets each person know you
especially notice his or her presence.

Calling names is also important when you give credit. Throwing
out group praise is not nearly so meaningful as specific compliments
for a job well done to the specific well doer.

Finally, calling names helps in communicating instructions. Jesus
found it necessary to zero in on the disciples and offer an invitation
by name. As church leaders and workers, our efforts succeed more

often when we, too, are specific in asking for help or assigning tasks.

The same phenomenon occurs around my house. If I make a statement like, "The garage should be cleaned out on Saturday," it gets about as much attention as announcing that the streets should be kept free of crime or that the azaleas should be in bloom next month.

When giving instructions to your family or your colleagues, call names if you want action.

D—Details

Be careful to get the details along with the big picture. Much of communication is expectation; we hear what we expect to hear. We catch a general idea and assume the details to match.

But when someone gives directions, relates a problem, presents a decision, or rejects a proposal, improve your understanding by getting all the details. Ask: Specifically, what do you mean? Like what? For instance? Are there any exceptions? How much? How often? When? Where? Why? How? Who? So what does that mean exactly for you? For me? Don't assume; dig.

E—Emotional Intimacy

You must establish emotional intimacy before someone can really level with you. Talking to some people is like crashing into pavement. Every comment is questioned or challenged; every feeling is denied or judged inappropriate; every offered confidence is met with silence.

Recall the feeling you get when you zip into a parking space a little too fast and far and bounce your front tires off the curb? There's a sudden jolt, you look around to see if anyone is watching, and you regret the wear to your tires. The same is true when you bump your honest self—basic feelings, inner conflicts or problems—into a person who sits like a cement curb and watches you bounce off.

Chris Kleinke in his book *First Impressions* cites several studies showing that we tend to like people who disclose medium amounts of themselves to us. Those who refuse to share little more about themselves than name, rank, and serial number, put us off and make it difficult to share more emotionally important things. Yet too much intimate self-disclosure makes others equally uncomfortable—particularly self-disclosure about shortcomings. Research also shows that the more we reveal of our emotions to others, the more they will reveal to us. But unfortunately, studies also show that people are often willing to disclose a lot more of their emotions to a stranger than to someone they know.[2] In other words, it's like bumping into the curb—we don't want anyone we know to see us hurting emotionally because we would be embarrassed if they bumped us away. Therefore, it's easier to disclose to a stranger and to talk about the weather with someone we know.

But Jesus' command to bear each other's burdens can only be carried out if we are willing to make an emotional connection. Jesus himself wept at Lazarus' death because of his emotional connection to Mary and Martha and the sorrow they felt—even though he knew he would restore Lazarus to life again. That emotional touching of another person is basic if we are to communicate with others as Jesus taught.

C. S. Lewis, the great Christian writer, wrote in *The Four Loves*: "Friendship is born at the moment when one person says to another, 'What! You too? I thought that no one but myself. . . . '"[3] Deep down inside our emotional selves, God has created us from the same image, the same emotional mold. When we share the hurt of a relationship that has ended through divorce or death or moving or betrayal, we all feel essentially the same pain. When we accomplish a lifelong dream or goal, we feel the same joy. The most personal, intimate feelings are those shared by all humanity. Therefore, the more we are willing to tell another person the intimacies of our lives, the more they can empathize and share our joys and burdens.

But, of course, we can become so submerged in someone emotionally that we can't separate from that person and live our own lives. That's the case when grown children can't leave a parent to unite emotionally with a wife or husband. And certainly that emotional leaving is a part of God's plan for our lives when we marry.

That brings us to the conclusion that emotional intimacy is basic for the deepest levels of communication—intimate friends, family, mate. Second, emotional intimacy is not only a possibility because we are all created in God's image, but a commandment for certain relationships. For our part, we must be willing to share our inner selves in emotional forthrightness before the other person will do the same.

And if you keep "bouncing off" someone in your life who refuses to share this intimacy, perhaps the difficulty is in your approach to his curb. Continue to bare more of your emotions inch by inch until he or she is willing to reciprocate. Start by sharing the little things: describe a household, work, or pastime project; tell a funny story on yourself; relate something that happened in your childhood that still affects the way you look at the world; mention someone you admire and explain why; mention a goal you'd like to achieve in the next ten years. Slowly, but safely, you will ease into that emotional intimacy that nurtures solid relationships.

F—Feedback

Actively solicit feedback from people to verify that they heard what you intended to communicate. You've read the sign, "I know you think you heard what you thought I said, but I'm not sure you understand that what you thought I said was not what I meant."

Instructors in active listening train students to repeat back to the speaker what was said until the speaker verifies that the hearer got the message right. Obviously, if we practiced this technique, we'd have a lot more conversations that lasted far into the wee hours. So we generally ignore the idea until we're trying to convey important details like telephone numbers, addresses, or the spelling of names, which we repeat to make sure we have them right.

But often in far more meaningful conversations, we fail to solicit any feedback at all and risk serious misunderstandings. You can hear the uncertainty with which many of us communicate in our use of tag phrases and questions at the end of our statements: "Do you know what I mean?" "Do you understand?" "Get what I'm driving at?" And, of course, to all these, the listener usually nods his head and says yes—whether he understands or not. This is *not* true feedback.

A listener will usually say that he understands, because he has been trained to say so all his life. From elementary school, you hear the teacher say, "Now I want you to do your best on this assignment; do you understand?" Everyone nods. When a speaker asks a listener if he understands, the listener thinks, *Of course I understand, I'm no dummy.* He's anxious to please.

Therefore, it's up to you, the speaker, to seek feedback actively and to be positive the other person gets your message. When you give instructions for doing a task, you don't ask a general, "Do you understand?" Instead, ask specifically: "Do you understand why I want you to use the new plugs? Do you remember why we are setting June 15 as the deadline?" In the case of elaborate instructions, ask someone to repeat them back to you so that you can verify accurately step by step. And when you uncover something that the person did not receive correctly, assume the blame: "No, that's not exactly right; *I* didn't make myself clear." Not. "No, *you* don't understand. *You* didn't hear me correctly."

When working with others, such as a committee or project group, plan time for formal feedback. Ask individuals and the group as a whole how you're coming across. But don't expect much response from general solicitations like: "Am I coming across?" They will answer yes and you're still no closer to knowing if they really understand or agree with you. Again, get specific: "Am I giving enough background?" "Are we on target with these time arrangements?" "Is everybody happy with the decision to spend the money?"

Also, be alert to nonverbal feedback that people can't or won't put into words. Tardiness to a meeting may indicate that the person is not eager to be present, that all is not going to suit her. Downcast eyes may be her way of expressing disagreement with what you've just said.

Finally, to ensure that you keep on getting valuable feedback, reward people when they say what they think. Listen to Jesus when he sought feedback from the disciples about their understanding of his divinity; " 'But what about you?' he said to them. 'Who do you say that I am?' Simon Peter answered, 'You? You are Christ, the Son of the living God!' 'Simon, son of Jonah, you are a fortunate man indeed!' said Jesus, 'for it was not your own nature but my Heavenly Father who revealed this truth to you!'" (Matt. 16:15-17, Phillips).

Often, we do just the opposite; we get angry with a "wrong" answer. Your teenager asks if he can have a friend over for the weekend and you go into a discussion of your plans, ending with eighteen reasons why company is out of the question. A little later in the day, the teen may comment that he feels you don't like having his friends around. Your first reaction may be anger, or astonishment, that he twists your words around and refuses to understand your work load. Such a reaction teaches the teen not to give you feedback at all in the future, not to check out his perceptions to see if they're correct.

Let others feed back so you can straighten out. In other words, don't imitate the potentates of old who killed the messengers who brought them bad news. If the feedback reveals a misinterpretation of what you said, be glad for the chance to reexplain and correct.

G—Genuineness

To be a good communicator, you must be genuine, showing the same face to all people all the time. Remember what it's like to be in a crowd miles from home and think you see someone familiar across the way, but you're not sure enough to call out and chance a mistake?

That's the same feeling you get when you try to carry on a conversation with a person who won't turn his emotional and mental face toward you. You think you know him, then you don't. There's always that hesitancy to call out to him, for fear he's really a stranger, not what he seems or says he is.

Recently my husband and I joined a group of friends for a late night snack after a concert. They had been impressed by the soloist and commented on her rapport with the audience. I couldn't join in their conversation, and, in fact, had trouble realizing that we were thinking of the same person.

Because I had arrived at the worship center early, I'd overheard the conversation between the singer and the sound-system people.

She had lambasted them because they had had trouble getting the equipment set up and hadn't allowed her enough time to practice. Further, she had threatened not to sing and to "leave them without a program at all."

When she stood to sing, smiled warmly, and made her opening remarks, "I'm so grateful for the chance to be here tonight. You're such a gracious people," I tuned out. You may have experienced the same disappointment when hearing a speaker who on the podium seems open, warm, and approachable but afterward, in conversation, is distant, arrogant, uninterested.

Notice the difference between a child's and an adult's attitude toward talking to a circus clown. The child delights in and warms to the clown's attempts at conversation, while the adult seems embarrassed or reticent. The adult feels much more comfortable if the clown pulls off the mask and talks face to face. We erect these same barriers when we aren't willing to show our genuine selves.

H—Humor

Humor can lift people up or knock them down, ease or create tension, display cleverness or reveal hostility, make a bad situation better or a heavy disagreement lighter.

Not all of us can have a quick wit, but we can develop a sense of humor in our communication. Wit is an intellectual sharpness; the ability to turn a phrase, play a word, crack a punch line. But humor has much more to do with the emotion and personality. Although it *can* mean cracking jokes, a sense of humor involves seeing the amusing side to life, laughing at yourself, relaxing in others' presence.

But humor based on wit can become a destructive tool to get even with others, to tear them down in an effort to raise self, to send someone a hostile message you wouldn't dare say on the level. Wit and humor, however, never fully cover hostility; the barbs still stick through and others become uncomfortable in their presence.

If you find yourself in the company of someone who employs humor as a weapon, it is a good idea to confront him with a comment that unveils the anger. "I get the idea from your last comment that you don't agree with the decision we just made. Do you want to talk about your opposition?" Or, "Under that bit of humor, I feel a note of seriousness. Have I offended you in some way? Would you like to talk about it?" Even if the person doesn't admit his hostility and take up your effort to discuss the issue, you have let him and others observing the scene know that you see through the disguise.

Finally, be careful at exactly what spot in the conversation you apply your wit or humor. Jokes on race, religion, or politics often offend others; don't use them indiscriminately. And always be careful that you never tease someone unless you are positive you have not chosen a sensitive spot. Some bald men crack jokes about their "dome," while others may smile but inwardly cringe when you do so.

When in doubt, don't. Let your humor be an asset, not a liability.

I—Inferences

Be aware of subtleties you imply, and inferences you make. Young children often have trouble distinguishing between fact and fiction as they watch television and read books. And even in adulthood, some people have trouble separating fact from inference.

Even the subjunctive-mood sentence construction (subjunctive-mood—contrary to fact: "If Mary *were* going to be in town, she would drop by to see you.") has dropped out of our everyday spoken language. Instead, we make declarative sentences carry both fact and inference. For example, "I saw Brenda's car parked in front of the Parkers' house all afternoon." That's a factual statement that allows for many inferences. Did Brenda have car trouble? Did Brenda baby-sit for the Parkers? Does he mean that Brenda and the Parkers must have finally confronted each other about their disagreements?

I once worked with an individual who never made any effort to understand the implications of what he said or the possible inferences of what others said to him. His motto was, "I say what I mean and I assume others do the same." That is, it was his motto until the following incident transformed his simplistic way of looking at communication.

He was overseeing the education program when a middle-aged couple, active in the church, became distant and uncooperative, and, finally, openly critical of his efforts in just about every area. After two or three attempts to discuss the problem with them, the relationship did not improve. Finally, due to their efforts, his job was in danger.

Then a mutual friend, observing the difficulty and mounting tension, stepped into the conflict as mediator. After a lengthy discussion with the couple, the core of the problem came to light. It seems that the couple's grown daughter, who had been teaching in one of the Bible study classes, had suddenly separated from her husband and moved out of the city without giving anyone any notice or explanation of her absence at the class.

Two weeks later, my friend got word through the grapevine that the woman would not be back and that he needed to find a teacher replacement. Short of teaching manuals, he had then made the following statement to the woman's parents, "I got word that Edna is giving up her class. When you talk to her, would you find out if she still has the teaching manual? We're short on books and I need to locate it for a new teacher."

In the conversation with the mediator, it seems that the couple had made several inferences from his brief statements: that their daughter should not have left her husband, that she was irresponsible for shirking her teaching duties and not letting him know, and that she had "stolen" the teaching book! These inferences had been the basis of their growing hostility toward my friend. He learned his lesson; factual statements are not always taken at face value.

When you hear a message, watch your own inferences. Did the teacher actually *say* that your child was incapable of learning algebra, or that she hadn't been turning in assignments? Did the boss actually *say* that your work was inferior, or that one letter should be rewritten? Did the neighbor *mean* that she didn't welcome your drop-in visit, or that this particular day was inconvenient?

Problems also surface when people make inferences from things they see or hear and then pass them on to you as fact. Be sure to ask for specifics; distinguish between the two.

Before sending your message, think in terms of results. How will the other person take what I'm going to say? Is he or she particularly sensitive about this matter? What will he think I mean by this statement? Be careful to word your message so that what you imply is what the other person infers, and listen carefully to see that what you infer is what the person actually means. Confusing? Ignore inferences altogether and see just how confusing things can get!

J—Judging

Refrain from putting a stopper on communication by being too quick to judge another's problem, idea, or behavior and too quick to fix it with solutions. Particularly troublesome are statements that begin like the following: "You know what you should do?" "You really ought to. . . ." "That happened to me once, and I can tell you right now that. . . ." "You know what your problem *really* is?" "Let me tell you how to. . . ."

Talking with someone who's ready to offer solutions before you've fully expressed the situation and your feelings about it is like calling the doctor when you have a fever and having him tell you to take two aspirins and go to bed.

Also, remember that judging reveals more about the judge than the person you're discussing. Describe actions or ask for changes, but don't hand out life sentences, at least until you've heard all the witnesses and examined the evidence.

K—Keeping Proper Distance

Have you ever noticed that when talking with certain people, you find that you've inched your way back and forth across the room? Chances are that one of you has made the other feel uncomfortable by not keeping proper spatial distance. Edward T. Hall describes four zones we use in communicating with others.

Patting someone on the back, letting a friend cry on your shoulder, or kissing your spouse represents *intimate* distance—touching range. *Personal* distance is from one to four feet apart, when most conversations are private and not meant to be overheard.

Social distance, about four to twelve feet apart, is comfortable for conversing with others when we don't mind if others overhear our small talk—at a party, greeting each other at worship service, or meeting at the shopping mall. *Public* distance, further than twelve feet apart, is when we tell our children, "Don't shout; he'll see us and come over in a minute." We use public distance to establish formality and control when speaking before a large group.[4]

Keeping improper spatial distance creates tension between people. You know the slight uneasiness and breathless quiet that you experience in a crowded elevator, even standing beside a close friend. And even husband and wife apologize when they accidently touch each other in the hallway. Not only do you get sprayed by people who spit, or cringe from their halitosis, you feel emotionally uncomfortable if someone stands too far away from you to inquire about a particular personal problem. You're afraid others will overhear. Once you recognize that some people lack discretion, you'll tend to guard what you say to them next time for fear of their bringing up the subject again at an indiscreet distance.

For others, the problem is standing too close, touching and hugging when the other person feels that the relationship is not so intimate. This becomes a problem particularly in religious circles where some are huggers and "holy kissers" and others are not.

Be aware of making others feel uncomfortable when you stand too close or touch inappropriately; if they inch away, don't follow them.

L—Limp Language

Watch your language for fuzzy words—the abstractions, dazzlers, and weasels: "*Similar* churches have tried this plan." What's *similar*? In size? In location? In potential? In educational or occupational makeup?

Meaning comes from people, not necessarily from the words they use. If you ask someone to do something "in a few days" and you have no deadline in mind, there's no problem. On the other hand, if you ask for a decision "in a few days" and actually have in mind Friday, you're setting yourself up for disappointment or anger if the other person doesn't operate on the same timetable as you.

In your own speech, try for simplicity, specificity, and clarity. Say "I want" not "we want." Don't hide behind "we're not getting the *support* we need," when you mean, "we need for you to attend this meeting." Rather than "the group should be disbanded," say, "in my opinion, the group should be disbanded." Say what you mean. Strive to express rather than impress. Use short, clear, unambiguous words.

M—Millions of Topics, Millions of Methods

Millions of topics and many methods are at your disposal to encourage conversation with difficult-to-talk-to people. Don't necessarily cross people off your list if they seem untalkative. Possibly, they only need help with conversational skills and encouragement.

You can oblige, first, by your body language; look at the person and, with your body posture, show that you are available to talk. You can even describe the other person's body language as an invitation to conversation: "You look rather disappointed; were you hoping that the decision would go the other way?" "You look excited. Is this the first time you've visited the area?" "You look uncomfortable. These chairs aren't too inviting, are they?"

To start a conversation, you may either state your opinion about something and then ask the other person what he thinks, or ask the other person what he thinks and then state your opinion. You can ask for directions or instructions, express an opinion or ask a question about a mutual acquaintance, an event, a habit, a hobby, a household problem. Like a journalist, think of the five W's: who, what, when, where, why.

And don't forget to really listen to what the person says; probe further to keep the conversational ball rolling. "In what ways do you mean?" "How come?" "Why do you think that always happens?"

You don't have to agree or to argue if your opinions differ. Simply say: "That's interesting. I hadn't thought of it that way before." Or, "That's a new idea. I'll have to give that some more thought." Be careful that your tone shows respect and acceptance, and you should be set to continue the relationship on other occasions.

In general, don't assume that because someone is quiet or doesn't have much to say to you, he isn't interested in knowing you. Perhaps he only needs encouragement or know-how to communicate more than the perfunctory remarks.

N—Neutral Statements

Neutral statements can be dangerous:
"The meat loaf has more tomato sauce than usual."
"You don't like it?"

"The rehearsal didn't begin until 8:45."
"Well, it wasn't my fault. Nobody was here on time. I couldn't start without the solos, could I?"

In his book *How to Manage Your Boss*, Christopher Hegarty recommends that you make the positive statements or give the reasons first, then follow with the neutral to avoid the preceding miscommunications:[5]

"This meat loaf is especially good. It has more tomato sauce than usual."

"I had a flat tire on the way, but I made it on time anyway. The rehearsal didn't begin until 8:45."

Makes all the difference in the world, doesn't it?

O—Open Yourself

Be open to new ideas and insights. Many times we fail even to get to first base in communicating with someone, because we never fully open our minds to what he's trying to say. See if you recognize any of the following attitudes in your own listening habits:

I-don't-understand listening.—You don't pay attention because you think the subject is over your head, and you're not interested enough to put forth the effort to listen and learn.

I-know-what-you-mean listening.—You assume you know what the other person thinks or feels, based on one thing he's said or on your own experience in a similar situation.

I've-got-my-mind-made-up listening.—You already know what you want to believe and don't want him to confuse you with more, possibly contradictory, details. While he's still talking, you concentrate on your rebuttal.

That's-off-the-wall listening.—You make a snap judgment, refusing to listen to unusual ideas, plans, opinions, or feelings.

I-don't-want-to-get-involved listening.—You mean, don't tell me your problems; I've got my own. You want to hear only the facts and to get on with the practical things that specifically affect you.

I-don't-like-you listening.—You don't like the way someone dresses, walks, looks, chews gum, so you're closed to anything she says, no matter what.

It takes a good force of will to erase your slate of preconceived ideas and habits and to give the other person's message a fair hearing.

P—Proper Place and Time

Be sufficiently sensitive to involve others in serious communication only at the proper place and time; meeting someone in a department store and striking up a conversation about his runaway daughter is insensitive. Check for privacy and choose a time that you will not be interrupted.

Q—Questions

Use them appropriately. Some people can ask about your weight, will, or wisdom tooth and you'd answer without hesitancy, while others can ask if you ride or walk to work and you begrudge them the information. Why?

People offend when they don't recognize what questions and information are approriate for what levels of relationships. As I explained in my earlier book *Making Friends with Yourself and Other Strangers*,[6] an *acquaintance* is someone you pass every day in the cafeteria, the lady whose son plays on the same ball team as yours, the man who delivers your firewood and occasionally stays to talk a few minutes. Usually, you don't go out of your way to strike up a conversation with this person, and you would have to look up his phone number or address.

Casual friends are those people who share a special interest or common purpose with you: the lady who sings alto beside you in the choir, the other mother who will be organizing the PTA carnival along with you, the family across the street with whom you play driveway basketball. You wouldn't have much to talk about with these people if this one activity dropped out of your life.

Close friends are those people you enjoy being around no matter what; you eat, play, shop, study, talk Bible and politics, or simply "hang around" together when you want to relax. You're not afraid of revealing personal opinions for fear of creating arguments or of finding yourself the subject of later gossip. These people laugh and cry with you.

Intimate friends are harder to come by; most people have no more than two or three such friends during a lifetime. This friend has the freedom to tell you the truth for your own good and feels it his duty whether you like it or not. He has the freedom to correct your character and cares that you reach your life goals. This person would forfeit a Caribbean cruise to stay home with you if your mother died.

Being unaware of these levels of friendship, people often make the mistake of asking questions that others consider prying and personal. If another person invades your privacy in this manner, don't hesitate to use silence to avoid answering the question. Or simply say something like, "Pardon me for not answering, but I don't really feel like talking about that. Would you mind if we changed the subject?" Or, "Why do you ask that?" Or, "I haven't given it much thought; what about you?"

On the other side of the coin, be aware of invading someone else's privacy by asking about things that they seem reluctant to share. If you genuinely want to try to expand a relationship to a deeper level, rather than ask questions of the other person and risk offending, be willing to share that same confidential information about yourself, leaving it to the other person to reciprocate. If he doesn't, you know he's not ready to move the relationship further into intimacy. When in doubt, let the other person broach the subject.

Other inappropriate questions fall into the category of showcase questions; they are designed to get a short response from the other person and to allow you the opportunity to showcase your own expertise. Most people see through this dishonest way of approaching a subject. If you'd like to contribute your superior insight on occasion, do so simply and honestly: "You know, I once made a study of _____ and found some really valuable ideas. One thing I learned was. . . . "

Another question type to avoid is the one that makes hidden statements. "Did you say that you were going to keep us here all day for this one project?" meaning, "I think that's too long (or ridiculous)." Don't be surprised that the hearer takes offense, even with your disclaimer: "Well, I was only asking." Most people know why you are "only asking" and what you mean to convey with the question.

Finally, watch questions that make the other person feel trapped: "You do want me to be able to finish this deal, so we can take our vacation, don't you?" If you say yes, then it follows you must keep quiet about the long hours your husband is away from home that week. Also, you make the other person feel trapped when you ask questions to which you already know the answer: "Johnny, I'm going to ask you one more time, did you leave my tools outside this morning?" If you're asking only to verify that you've got the situation straight, say so.

Don't hesitate, however, to ask questions that encourage further thought or reflection on the other person's part on a neutral subject. The idea is not to avoid questions altogether, but simply to avoid questions on subjects inappropriate to your particular relationship or questions that trap or insult or brag.

R—Reflect Feelings

Reflect feelings, not just facts. Some, who for years have heard about reflective listening, feel awkward when they actually do it, feeling that they sound silly. But usually that's the case only when the person reflects facts:

"I left early in the morning, thinking he would be anxious to see me. But when I arrived, he wasn't even home."

"You left early in the morning. You thought he would be anxious for you to get there, but he wasn't home."

This kind of parroting and reflection is valuable in checking factual details, but little else. Deeper communication takes place when you reflect feelings:

"I left early in the morning, thinking he would be anxious to see me. But when I arrived, he wasn't even home."

"You were excited about a big reunion, huh? And then disappointed that he wasn't home."

"Well, no, not exactly disappointed. Although I guess I was that, too. But I really think I was more angry than anything. He'd made me believe that my coming was the most important thing he had on his mind and instead of waiting to see if I would show, he decided to go skiing with another friend."

"I can see why you felt angry then, even embarrassed."

"Yes, very embarrassed."

You can see from this dialogue how reflecting feelings helps you clarify and correct your own assumptions. It also helps the other person discover and reflect on his own feelings and feel understood and released, as if he has communicated, rather than simply talked with you.

S—Silence

Don't be afraid of silence. Singers learn to pause after a dramatic ending to an anthem or solo to let the audience reflect on the message. Remember Jesus' dramatic use of silence when he knelt to write on the ground and waited for the mob around the adulterous woman to reflect on his words about who should cast the first stone.

Silence gives the other person a chance to collect his thoughts, to see where a conversation has been, and to consider where he'd like it to go next. If you have to do something while you wait, nod your head or smile. Give the other person time to reflect and then continue. Use a probe question if you think it necessary to show him you're still interested: "Why do you think you feel that way? What do you plan to do now? How can you improve the situation?"

The old cliche "silence is golden" is true not only because its opposite is irritating, but also because in a positive way silence gives golden opportunity for sharing on a deeper, emotional level.

T—Total Meaning

Look for the total meaning in someone's message. Frequently, we answer the intent of someone's words rather than only the content.

Two friends accidently encounter each other in the library; one says, "You didn't go to the wedding shower for Marjorie?" If the first friend answered the question literally, she'd say, "No, silly, I'm standing here talking to you."

But the intent of the message was, "I'm surprised you didn't go to the wedding shower for Marjorie. Didn't you get an invitation?" Or, "Is something wrong?" Perhaps, "I thought you were planning to attend the wedding shower. What came up to make you change your plans?"

Social researchers estimate that no more than 15 to 35 percent of the real meaning of our social sharing comes from words; 65 to 85 percent of our message is conveyed by nonverbal signals.[7] Some people think that they only communicate when they're conscious of doing so. But, as I mentioned earlier, it's a big mistake, to assume that people mean only what they say or say only what they mean. Many of the conversations between you and your teen about dating have little to do with dating and a lot to do with the trust between parent and child. Likewise, many conversations about eighteen-wheelers may have little to do with trucks and a lot to do with power politics and someone's self-concept.

Always examine the total meaning of someone's words so that you can communicate fully: What details did he or she choose to give? To omit? Why did he repeat a certain idea several times? In what context did he say it? What did her facial expression say? When words and body language conflict, trust the body language; it's harder to fake.

U—Undivided Attention

Give it liberally; attend with your whole body. You remember sitting in a classroom when the teacher said to the class, "Pay attention now," as she explained something on the chalkboard. Although no one may have been disruptive by talking, her comment was probably prompted by the class' body language; they slumped away from her and let their eyes drift to more important concerns. You know the same feeling when you talk to someone who keeps looking over your shoulder or her own, as if looking for more exciting action elsewhere.

Art Linkletter in his book *Yes, You Can* relates an incident with the then California Governor Jerry Brown that impressed him significantly about giving full attention. Both were scheduled to speak at a meeting for narcotics officers, and Linkletter says he didn't care for the governor because of his political policies. But Brown stopped by to say hello to Linkletter before the meeting began. "He kept standing beside me, asking probing, intelligent questions about my attitude toward drug abuse. For the five minutes that we talked, he gave me his total, undivided attention. He didn't look around but looked directly into my eyes. He acted as though we were completely alone, without another soul anywhere in hearing."

Linkletter goes on to explain that Brown made no play of expansive rhetoric for the onlookers and that the short conversation was probably the most dramatic change in attitude he'd ever made about anyone. "He had turned me around purely because of his marvelous ability to listen to what I had to say and to make me feel important through his attentiveness."[8]

I'm not talking about a fake display of attention, but rather genuine concentration on what the other person is saying—no interruptions, no topic switches to suit your own interests, no perfunctory comments. When a listener shifts his eyes back and forth, shuffles his feet, as if to make an escape, or makes ho-hum responses, communication stops and only the words continue.

V—Voice Tones and Volume

Solomon knew the power of both: "A soft answer turneth away wrath" (Prov. 15:1). Voice tones and volume reveal much about personality, problems, and your enthusiasm for the conversation at hand. A loud voice can express anger or excitement and a soft voice can convey sadness or joy. But volume coupled with tone leaves no doubt in your listener's mind about how you feel about what you're saying. If you don't believe how much these two components affect your message, recall a movie which has actors speaking in a foreign language with no translation provided; their volume and tone convey the entire message and few listeners have trouble understanding it.

How important is volume? Some people's voices are about as pleasant as a chain saw—harsh, loud, brash, demanding attention.

A few years ago I surveyed 215 teens for a book on friendship, asking them to list some traits that they considered obnoxious in other people. I was surprised to find that a vast number of them mentioned that someone who was a "loudmouth" turned them off. Even adults tend to shy away from a consistently loud voice that seems to involve them in unwanted negative attention.

Others squeak up with the volume of a mouse, and, unfortunately, they are frequently judged to be timid or even boring or incompetent. As a result, they get little attention—unless, like their furry counterparts, they happen to run over somebody's foot.

On the same friendship survey, I asked respondents what they thought of timid, quiet people who had trouble speaking up. Overwhelmingly, they expressed impatience. Most of the comments echoed this one: "I make an attempt to talk to them; but if they don't snap out of it soon, that's their problem. I go my own way and ignore them." Someone who mumbles, in effect, says to others: "I'm not worth listening to." And most receivers are unwilling to work too hard to communicate.

If you often feel that others overlook you, talk over you, or shy away from your loudness, you might try to record your speaking voice and see what warmth or lack of warmth your tone and volume convey. Then with or without trained help, you can consciously work toward developing enthusiasm and energy in your voice without becoming a loudmouth.

W—Weigh Your Words

As she sat at dinner one night, my young daughter, exasperated about a friend of hers who'd told a secret, complained: "Everything that goes in her ears comes out her mouth."

Think before you speak: Is it true? Is it necessary? Is it helpful? Is there another way to say it that would be more tactful? What implications will my words have for the other person? Will I regret what I've said in the warm light of God's presence?

X—Exaggeration (*I cheated*)

Exaggeration has no place in true communication. When you exaggerate to make a point, the point often gets lost in the listener's exasperation at your method. You remember the fable about the shepherd boy who cried "wolf" so many times that he could arouse no ally in his time of need. When we continually exaggerate wants to needs, needs to crises, or simple actions to daring feats, we run out of words and emotions to convey our true feelings or facts.

Exaggeration may work for the stand-up comic, but it undercuts the rest of us.

Y—Yield

Yield to speaking signals of the other person. Mary Parlee Brown writing in *Psychology Today* has outlined some of the general rules of conversation that apply to our American culture. One rule is that the speaker signals his intention to yield the floor. He may do this by stopping at the end of a sentence, by dropping his pitch or volume level, or by using such body language as turning his eyes away or shrugging his shoulders as in "I give up."[9]

Another unwritten rule is that the speaker indicates that he wants a response by addressing the other person by name, by asking a direct question, or by making eye contact.

Someone who doesn't learn these rules unconsciously has a hard time conversing with others. The other person never knows when he is finished speaking or if he wants a response at all.

You've had the same experience if you've ever told the punch line to a joke that no one caught. You feel as though you are dangling in mid-air waiting for the other's brain to compute. The same is true of the person who doesn't yield the floor effectively. When the listener misses a cue to respond, the speaker often feels that what he said was uninteresting or that the other person did not wish to continue the communication. Either way, they both lose out on what might have been a worthwhile sharing together.

Z—Zero in on Others

Focus on the other person, not yourself. Salespersons know that they're much more successful with customers if they can get the customer to talk about himself and his own needs as he perceives them. Even small children come alive when all the attention in the room is directed toward them; they begin to play to the audience for all its worth. To get to know someone else and make him feel significant to you, zero in on his interests, his family, his problems, and his goals, Eventually he'll become interested enough in you to make it a fifty-fifty communication and to ask you for the same information.

Regardless of how much you take these ABC's to heart, you will not have learned the whole game of communication in one lesson. And even if you were to practice all the techniques and attitudes described here, all your communication efforts still might not be successful or pleasant.

Why? Communication involves risk. Remember, I said that communication couldn't be a one-way affair. Your listening may be unappreciated or exploited; someone may take advantage of your generosity of spirit and use you for a comfortable crying towel, wring you out emotionally, and then never reciprocate when the time comes for a listener in your life.

Or communication may lead to self-discovery about your inconsistencies and improper attitudes. You may hear criticism and come to see yourself as another person sees you—in an unfavorable light. That self-examination may call for forgiveness, effort, and change on your part.

Finally, honest communication makes you vulnerable to a deeper commitment to the other person. Once you've seen someone's emotional ingrown toenails, it's hard to make him wear tight, stereotypical shoes. You want to offer surgery and/or salve to ease the pain and improve his mobility.

But no one would argue against the fact that the benefits outweigh the risks of communication. To understand and to be understood is one of the greatest liberating forces in life. Jesus understood our bondage and came to set us all free to abundant living.

Take the gift; learn to bridge the gap to better relationships by more effective communication.

3

"You're dead-wrong"

How to Disagree Without Being Disagreeable

Do you recall the is/is-not arguments of childhood, when you and a peer finally had to appeal to a higher authority—a teacher or parent—to set the record straight? And do you recall the triumph of being pronounced right and the humiliation of being wrong?

From preschool forward, children pick up the idea that those who disagree with them are enemies, because they cause that pain. They also learn that those who agree make them feel good; therefore, they become friends. The name of the game, then, becomes making more friends than enemies—or agreeing more and disagreeing less. As a result, disagreement becomes a lifelong snare on the path to potentially rewarding relationships.

As adults we need to learn to look at disagreement in a new light. First of all, we need to understand that two sides can be right. I remember the first time two high school seniors came to me as a teacher and said, "You goofed, Mrs. Booher." Comparing test grades and answers, they found that both had received 100 percent credit for their answers to the essay question—and they had given opposite answers. Amused at their shocked expressions, I explained that no, I had not goofed this time in grading their papers, that both answers were right because the essay had been an opinion question and they had both supported their opinions with reasons.

Think about it: two sides may have equal merit. If nothing else, Paul's letters to the Romans and other churches organized around the world emphasize the multifaceted prongs of the gospel and its application. Romans 14 stands out as a chapter in which the concept of two sides being right is especially poignant.

Some think that Christians should observe the Jewish holidays as special days to worship God, but others say it is wrong and foolish to go to all that trouble, for every day alike belongs to God. On questions of this kind everyone must decide for himself. If you have special days for worshiping the Lord, you are trying to honor him; you are doing a good thing. So is the person who eats meat that has been offered to idols; he is thankful to the Lord for it; he is doing right. And the person who won't touch such meat, he, too, is anxious to please the Lord, and is thankful (5-6, TLB).

And yet, churches have split over how to accomplish a building program, as if there were only one way to do so. Some members insist that the Bible teaches a pay-as-you-go philosophy, that the church should "owe no man" and therefore borrow no money to build, and, finally, that if God wanted the church built, he'd provide the money beforehand. Others of the membership disagree that the Bible admonishes against borrowing, only against borrowing and not repaying the debt. Further, they insist that the more money they borrow, the greater pledge of faith shown in God's provision to repay the debt.

In still other situations, church members have insisted that the building should be the finest and most elaborate building Christians can construct, pointing to the example of Solomon's magnificent Temple, built to signify God's glory to the world. But people on the other side of the fence have asked, "Why the emphasis on the building, which is really for our own comfort, after all? Remember that when Jesus walked upon this earth, he had no place even to call his own home. The money from our tithes and offerings should be going to feed the hungry and clothe the poor, not to build a fancier-than-necessary church building."

To both sides, I would refer again to Romans 14. Both sides struggle to please the Lord. God is the judge of motives, not we ourselves. That is not to say that there are no moral absolutes, but simply that *many* things we disagree about have no right or wrong sides. The next time you feel the compulsion to "argue something through" until the other person "sees the light," remember that he may already be seeing the light, his own light.

Both sides can be right. It's a difficult concept, but one we, as adults, should begin to work to understand.

A second handle to catch hold of in matters of disagreement is the capacity to mentally, emotionally, and physically release people to be different. Jesus showed that understanding and that approval in his dealing with Mary and Martha. Martha was the type who fussed over Jesus and tried to show her love by seeing that he had a nice meal, that the house was clean and refreshing, that he had a fresh basin of water in which to soak his feet, and an aired mat to sleep on. Mary, on the other hand, showed her love by sitting at his feet, hanging on his every word, offering him conversation and encouragement by listening to the stories of his travels and ministry. But you'll notice that as many times as Jesus had visited in their home, he was not the one who initiated the conversation with Martha about household work. He did not ask her to show her love in the same way as Mary. His comments about Mary having chosen the "better part" came only at Martha's own insistence that he "speak to Mary" about not helping her. In other words, Martha had not released her sister to be different; Jesus had.

Paul speaks much to this attitude with his analogy of members of Christ's church and parts of a physical body all having different functions. Although the seven gifts Paul mentions in Romans 12:2-8 should be cause for unity, not dissension, the latter is frequently the case.

The choir director, who has the gift of administration, and is so organized that he knows what anthem the junior choir will sing March 14, 1995, complains that his wife, who has the gift of practical helps, spends too much time building the drama set, which she should have simply delegated to someone else. The widow who has the gift of mercy and spends Thursday mornings with residents at the nursing home, listening to their stories, hears criticism from the Bible teacher who can't understand why the widow isn't more faithful to Bible study sessions and isn't more anxious to hear his teaching on the Mosaic laws.

The gifts which Paul spoke of can never be unifying in our churches and in our homes until we release people to be different—

to have different motivations, to have different interests, to like catsup or mustard, as the case may be. Most of us don't have much trouble with the disputes about catsup or mustard; it's the money, manners, and motivation matters that lock us into conflict.

Another helpful approach to disagreement is to learn to separate your ego from your work, possessions, and opinions and to allow others to do the same. Proverbs 13:10 says: "Only by pride cometh contention . . . ." A coating of pride makes the blandest pill hard to swallow.

Consider for a moment a simple thing like driving down a residential street in your neighborhood with a group of strangers. The conversation turns to houses and architectural styles. As you pass by the different houses, various passengers in the car begin to comment on which styles they do and do not particularly like, pointing out landscapes and window coverings that either enhance or detract from the appearance.

When the group passes your house and begins to discuss your yard, your landscaping, your window coverings, the color of your trim, do you feel any different as you listen to the comments? Would you tend to offer explanations about why you chose the miniblinds that you have—which has nothing at all to do with the fact that the people in the car like or don't like them?

If we attach ego to insignificant things like material possessions, think how much more closely we tend to associate our work and our political, moral, and religious views with our personhood.

When I first began teaching business writing workshops for corporate clients, I noted the close tie between employees' egos and the writing tasks they performed each day on the job. Workshop participants frequently share with me the bitterness they feel toward supervisors who continually edit their memos or letters for what they consider no reason at all other than personal preference. To many, having a memo criticized and edited is no less offensive than being told that the supervisor doubts his or her basic honesty. Work has become so attached to ego that it vies as closely as personality traits for defining us.

Others who sense our inability to separate ego from opinions, possessions, and performance find it difficult to talk with us. They hesitate to give valuable feedback for fear of offending. Immediately that hesitancy creates two more problems in that it limits our opportunities to make something even more perfect, correct, or acceptable, and it also creates a pool of reservation around the continuing relationship.

Of course, the problem of not separating ego from position and performance is not always the fault of the person whose views and behavior you're discussing. In 1 Corinthians 1:11-17, it was members of the church congregation who had caused dissension by claiming to be followers of Apollos, Cephas, Christ, or Paul, according to who had baptized or preached to them. In this case, it wasn't the leaders themselves, but those who had received their help who created disharmony by making the whole issue one of personalities.

The same thing happens today when issues become associated with specific people. Fred stands up to express his opinion about assigning funds to project A, and then Sam speaks up to advocate budgeting support of project B. The following comments then become not a discussion of support for the projects but a discussion of Fred's plan versus Sam's plan. Simply by the way ideas are worded, issues become associated with individuals. And when one viewpoint loses, the person involved often feels (or is made to feel by "innocent bystanders") that the defeat is a personal one.

To the best of your abilities, strive to keep ego—yours and the other person's—separated from issues. As Paul told the Corinthian church, he was glad that he didn't baptize too many of them, because he didn't want any part of the "fan clubs" developing there. His purpose was to preach Christ and unity.

When dealing with disagreement, another consideration is to make sure the point merits the disagreement. Is your conflict worth calling attention to? We've just passed through a decade of "let it all hang out" and "tell it like it is." With such encouragement, what does one use for a measuring stick in determining what is and is not worth expressing disagreement?

Titus 3:9 outlines a few topics to avoid: "But avoid foolish questions, and genealogies, and contentions, and strivings about the law; for they are unprofitable and vain." In other words, avoid things that can't be settled definitively and that cause only harm, not good. Discussion of these issues won't improve a situation and appeal only to pride.

Jesus himself rejected this kind of nitpicking. When John reported to the Master that he'd seen another who didn't travel with their group casting out devils in Jesus' name, he said that he had told the man to stop. Jesus countered John, "Forbid him not: for he that is not against us is for us" (Luke 9:50). Why argue about the unimportant? If Jesus didn't get upset about someone using his name to verify his authority, why should we get annoyed over what color to paint the nursery?

A fifth consideration when handling disagreement is to remember that people don't necessarily like or respect those who always agree with them. King Ahab had his corner full of "yes men" when he wanted to go to war against Ramoth-gilead (1 Kings 22). But you remember that both he and his ally King Jehoshaphat couldn't rest with their decision until they called Micaiah, God's prophet, who was known for his disagreements with the king's plans. When he wanted a true, straight answer, King Ahab had little respect for the four hundred prophets who always predicted what he wanted to hear. Even today, managerial studies tell us that managers frequently have more respect for those who disagree with them, at least initially, than for the staff members who always say what they think the boss wants to hear.[1]

Often we condemn those who vote for a political candidate because of the way he combs his hair, shares the spotlight with his wife, or appears humble during press conferences. Yet some who condemn that superficial approach in politics take stands on other issues that are based on personalities, for fear of disagreeing with someone they don't want to alienate.

In keeping these five approaches to disagreement in mind, you can and should express disagreement to an advantage—to solve a problem, not create one. Disagreement should have little to do with friendship, personality, loyalty, or encouragement and everything to do with respect, truth, goals and purpose. He who can express and accept disagreement in such a light will profit in both his spiritual and secular pursuits.

The skill in using disagreement to advantage, then, involves expressing your difference in such a way so as not to offend but to cause the other person to rethink his position. The following guidelines offer help in expressing disagreement in that manner:

(1) *Reduce or expand the opposing idea to its ultimate end.*—That is, in a practical, calm manner lead the other person to see the full implications of what she is saying.

This was Jesus' manner when he responded to the mother of James and John about her sons having seats of authority on his right and left hands: "Ye know not what ye ask. Are ye able to drink of the cup that I shall drink of, and to be baptized with the baptism that I am baptized with?" (Matt. 20:22). "Think," he said, "what you're asking!"

Again, recall Jesus' attempt to wash the disciples' feet. Peter refused to submit to the washing, saying that he was unworthy and that the situation should be reversed. Jesus, however, announced the full implication for Peter to consider: "If I do not wash you, you have no part in me" (John 13:8, RSV). Peter quickly thought it over and reversed his position.

In similar situations of disagreement, you can use the same techniques Jesus used. Make a statement or ask a question that will cause the person to rethink the issue: "If we go with your plan now, Erma, to donate the use of the buildings to this organization, we will need to find a way to budget the additional custodial expenses involved. What are your suggestions on that?"

This nonthreatening manner will help Erma to see all that's involved in her original idea and may lead her to change her mind, or at least to modify her earlier position to accommodate objections or possible problems. This technique is so innocuous, in fact, that most people will not even realize your disagreement.

(2) *Examine the sources of the information.*—Perhaps the basis of disagreement is incorrect data and details. Such was the case when the Sadducees came to Jesus to ask him about the hypothetical case of the woman who married seven times. Trying to trap him, they

asked whose wife she would be in the resurrection. Jesus immediately focused on the basis of their dispute, the source of information: "But Jesus answered them, 'You are wrong, because you know
neither the scriptures nor the power of God. For in the resurrection
they neither marry nor are given in marriage, but are like angels in
heaven'" (Matt. 22:29-30, RSV). They had the wrong foundation for
their argument; the details were scrambled.

Although we cannot be so confident in tone as Jesus, we can
confide the basis for our opinion, thereby suggesting that the other
person do the same: "The reason I said it wasn't necessary to spend
that much money on costumes is that I talked with the school drama
teacher, who said the costumes for their recent production cost only
$900. . . . How exactly did you arrive at your $2,300 request figure?"

The following discussion of proper and improper funds should
then center around getting the most reliable information on which
to base a decision. Sharing sources is also a graceful way to let the
other person save face: "Perhaps you didn't have access to some of
the most recent figures that came in this month's XYZ report, but
one article said, . . . " lets the other person dismiss his previous idea
in favor of your more reliable source.

(3) *Use analogy.*—Make your disagreement, which may not be easily
understandable to the other person, more visual by making a com-
parison. Jesus used this method in comparing the rich man's attempt to
get into heaven to a camel crawling through the eye of a needle.

In your analogies to settle disagreement, try something like: "I
think the difference in these two computers is comparable to the
difference between a manual mimeograph and a copier that col-
lates." Or, "Attempting a project like this would be like trying to cut
my lawn with a pair of scissors. I don't think we'd ever make any
headway."

(4) *Use experience or history.*—Having no facts or sources of
information, you can always identify your own experience or that of
someone else as your basis for disagreement. Paul used this tack in
many of his witnessing experiences among Jews who held to the old
Jewish laws and rituals for their salvation. After identifying himself
as a "Jew of the Jews," he expounded on the personal experiences

that lead him to disagree with that old way of thinking. Personal experience and history are difficult to refute. Make sure, however, that your own personal experience has not blinded you to the possibility that your experience may have been rare and nonapplicable in a particular situation.

(5) *To avoid being taken into a dispute, talk "around" a subject rather than "through" it.*—Consider several of Jesus' examples of handling disagreement. Groups of scribes, chief priests and elders asked him about his authority for teaching and preaching. Instead of answering their questions, he asked them about John's baptism. Was it of heaven or of men? Of course, wanting to avoid that hot topic in front of the crowds, the scribes, chief priests, and elders held their tongues. Then Jesus skirted their original issue with: "Neither tell I you by what authority I do these things" (Luke 20:8).

Again, Jesus avoided discussing specifics and getting into a disagreement when he dealt with the men who brought him a coin and asked about paying taxes to Caesar. He made a general statement encompassing the right of both responsibilities: "Render therefore unto Caesar the things which are Caesar's; and unto God the things that are God's" (Matt. 22:21).

In your own dealings, particularly concerning the controversial and/or unimportant matters mentioned in Titus 3:9, make general statements that embrace both sides of the issue. And express your reluctance to give an opinion on anything that might be offensive to some and that certainly would serve no worthwhile purpose. People have no difficulty at all in "talking around" invitations to do volunteer work that they don't want to do, or "talking around" questions of salary or age.

If nothing else works to get around the issue, you can simply say: "I'd rather not express an opinion about that." Or, "I'd rather not commit myself to a position that I haven't given much thought to." Or, "I don't think we'll ever settle or agree on an issue like this." Or, on the light side, brush the question off with, "Next time I have two free weeks, maybe we'll get into that."

But do offer to listen to the other person's ideas if he or she seems anxious to express them. Often questions beginning, "What do you think about . . . " are only attempts to express one's own views. Rather than answer, simply invite the asker to tell you what he thinks.

(6) *Use a positive tone, and, when possible, emphasize areas of agreement.*—Because we have neither the wisdom nor the authority of Jesus in dealing with those who disagree, avoid outright contradictory statements such as "You're dead wrong about that." "You don't know what you're talking about, because. . . . " "Somebody told you a lie." "Listen, folks, you're on the wrong track." "I don't agree with you."

Instead, give the person credit for what he says and then state your opposing view in a positive way: "It's interesting that you should say that, because I got just the opposite feeling from reading the same article. I interpreted the author to mean. . . . "

"I'm glad you brought up that subject and your feelings about it. I, too, have been giving that a lot of thought, and while I don't quite see the situation as you do, I think we do agree that. . . . "

"I understand what you're saying, and (not *but*, which emphasizes contradiction) it also seems to me. . . . "

"You could be right. There's more than one way to look at the situation."

All these statements and phrases show acceptance of the other's opinion, while leaving opportunity to disagree in an agreeable way. When disagreeing, you want to sound like a court witness rather than the prosecutor or defender. That matter-of-fact manner takes the pressure off the other person to play judge and reach a decision about the issue.

When disagreement is only a matter of off-handed discussion, the effects are usually minimal. But when disagreement stands in your way of supporting or dismissing yourself from a group project, the effects are more profound on both you and the group.

A few years ago, a local church decided to sponsor a half-way house to attract drug-involved youth of the area who might not otherwise ever step inside a church building to hear the gospel. As soon as the church budgeted the money for the project, the youth group plunged into the effort of turning an old building on the church grounds into an attractive youth center.

Halfway through a long, hard summer of installing plumbing and rearranging partitions, a small group of parents, youth, and the church staff sat down to draw up a list of guidelines for appropriate building use and conduct for the half-way house opening. One of the results of the meeting was a restriction on the age of church youth who could staff the center. Because of the drug-addicted teens whom the center hoped to attract from the streets, some of the parents felt that staffing should be restricted to Christian teens over the age of fifteen.

One parent, however, whose thirteen-year-old son had been helping in the carpentry work disagreed, saying his son was mature enough to handle any problems that might arise. Refusing to abide by the overwhelming majority's opinion (even shared by younger youth on the guidelines committee), the father created quite a disturbance over the issue. Finally, unable to persuade enough people to join his rebellion, he decided to withdraw from the entire project and refused to let his still-willing son offer any more help with the renovation. Needless to say, his disagreement and eventual withdrawal had a serious effect on the group's morale.

When you're faced with disagreement in a group situation, your basic options are the same as those outlined in chapter 7, "Resolving Conflict." You can overpower, withdraw, or compromise. But even though you have the authority in the group to overpower and to force others to accept your position, you build resentment and the effort is often doomed to failure from the beginning. Others may sabotage your success.

Compromise in areas of disagreement (other than those involving moral issues), brings the best results in most cases. Remember, though, that compromise does not always mean meeting others halfway; it may mean that you'll travel 90 percent of the distance between you.

And if the group will not compromise, you have the option of dropping out altogether, like the child who says, "I'll just take my toys and go home." On the other hand, giving your enthusiastic support to the group's effort establishes you as an agreeable person who hates to disagree, rather than as a disagreeable person who happens to agree.

If disagreement seems to be a continual pattern in your life, rethink your approaches: remember that two sides can be right; release people to be different; separate your ego from your opinions or performance and allow others to do the same; make sure an issue is worth disagreeing over; and finally, remember that others don't necessarily respect or like you less simply because you disagree.

Making waves doesn't necessarily mean making enemies, if you know how to sail choppy waters. In fact, when you save someone from a costly mistake by expressing opposing views, you may turn disagreement into quite an agreeable relationship.

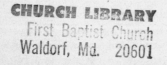

4

"If I were you, I'd. . . "

Giving and Receiving Advice

Brenda assembled the salad ingredients on the counter top as she tried to explain her indecision to Matty, her mother-in-law. "I've always said I was going back to school if we moved close enough to a college and if Charles thought we'd be around long enough for me to get a degree."

"Of course, you can't really have any assurance of that, can you?" her mother-in-law asked.

"Well, the chances look good, at least. Since we've just moved and since his supervisor said the project would take three to five years.

"Charles needs you to be free to host dinner parties and things like that, doesn't he? Studying takes a big chunk of time. It's not just the classroom time that's involved."

"But I'm always busy with something anyway. Painting the bedrooms, church projects," Brenda argued, as she peeled and diced the cucumbers.

"But you'd have to meet classes day in, day out," Matty countered. Brenda slid her knife along the thin stalks of celery, letting the strings fall into the sink. "After you've paid that tuition money, it's too late to change your mind and drop out."

Brenda looked up at her mother-in-law. "You've got me ready to quit before I've even started." Matty looked sheepish and took a seat at the table, out of her daughter-in-law's range of vision. Brenda continued, "If I went summers, I could finish in two years and have my teaching certificate."

"That means the kids are on their own then."

"Well, I'd say they're pretty much on their own anyway—at seventeen and eighteen. I'd be home by 3:30 or 4:00 every day."

"*If* you got your classes scheduled just like you want them every semester. Which would be highly unlikely, if you ask me."

"Maybe not."

"And a degree's no guarantee of a job nowadays. Teaching is an especially crowded field. Sure could turn out to be a waste of time."

Brenda sat the salad bowl on the table in front of Matty. "I take it you don't think my starting back to college would be a good idea?"

"Who, me? I'd never try to tell you what to do, dear. That's completely up to you."

Brenda tried to swallow a grin and sat down to lunch.

Giving

Have you ever had anyone say to you, "If you ask me, I think . . . ." and been tempted to interrupt, "But I didn't ask you"? Giving advice comes as naturally for some people as breathing. But when you're on the receiving end, you realize that more often than not what you really want is encouragement and moral support for your own reasoning, decisions, and actions.

Watch, particularly, the tendency to scrunch advice into what should be informational statements or stimulating questions:

Advice: "I think you should probably go ahead and start the meeting."

Information: "It's ten minutes past seven."

Advice: "I don't think you should ask Danielle out again since she changed her plans on you last time at the very last minute."

Probing question: "Does it bother you that Danielle waited until the last minute last time before telling you she'd made a change of plans?" (If it doesn't, hold the advice.)

Advice: "Don't you realize that if you're going to get a summer job, you'd better start applying in February?"

Information: "My supervisor at work told me this morning that most companies have already filled all their available summer jobs by February."

Advice: "I'd think twice before asking Fred to head that campaign."

Information: "Fred headed our campaign three years ago, and he resigned right in the middle of it without even giving us an explanation."

Other harmless forms of advice creep into our conversations when we may think we're actually comforting someone. We make comments like: "Just take it easy and relax. There's no reason to worry. Just do your best." Although, as with most advice, the intention is noble, the result is often that the person thinks you're not taking his predicament seriously.

If you have a sneaky feeling that such impromptu advice frequently drips from your lips, try to catch yourself in mid-sentence and retract. Gradually, you'll learn to muzzle the words before they come out.

But why not unsolicited advice? One of the biggest problems is that it makes the receiver feel inadequate and defensive. In effect, she takes the advice to mean that you don't think her capable of making the decision or working out the problem. And, of course, much advice begins with a statement of analysis like: "I've been watching you lately, and I . . . " or, "You're young, of course, and haven't had as much experience at this sort of thing, but. . . . " Few enjoy feeling like an insect under a microscope.

That is not to say that you should never give unsolicited advice. The Christian community today has made progress in its own growth and in evangelizing the world because prophets and preachers have given unsolicited advice down through the years. Sons and daughters have turned aside from devastating perils due to a parent's unsolicited warning. And adults have held and rebuilt their marriages or their businesses because someone cared enough to "interfere" with advice.

But the keys here to successful advising are *agreement of goals* and *willingness to hear*. Let's look at a couple of examples of necessary but unsolicited advice. In Exodus 18, Jethro, Moses' father-in-law, watched Moses as he sat from dawn to dusk judging disputes between the Israelites and applying God's laws to their problems. You'll notice that before Jethro began dispensing advice, though, he asked Moses *why* he was doing what he was doing.

In other words, Jethro didn't presume to have all the answers; he wanted to make sure he understood the facts, as well as Moses' intentions. When Moses told him that his only goal was that the people know God's laws, then Jethro advised him of a more effective way to reach his goal. Jethro suggested that Moses organize the people into groups and appoint rulers over them to help settle disputes more quickly. Because Moses was willing to hear what his father-in-law said and because Jethro understood and advised within the guidelines of Moses' own goals, Moses took and profited from the advice.

In another situation, the prophet Nathan "interfered" in family business to advise Bathsheba about having her son Solomon crowned king. First Kings 1 reveals that Nathan followed the same pattern as Jethro. He got the "facts" first. He asked Bathsheba if she were aware that David's other son, Adonijah, had had himself crowned and planned to take over the kingdom. Once he knew that Bathsheba still wanted her son Solomon crowned, he offered advice on how she could get the elderly King David to make that choice while he was still alive. Bathsheba bowed to Nathan's counsel because they agreed on goals.

So when you feel tempted to give unsolicited advice, first make sure that the person is in a receptive mood. Second, make sure that your advice is in keeping with that person's ultimate goals—new home, business degree, marriage, whatever.

Of course, you can be much freer with your counsel if someone sincerely *asks* for it. But if you take advice giving seriously—and you should—remember that your main role is to stimulate thinking. That means primarily pointing out alternatives and raising questions. You do not necessarily have "to have all the facts" or experience before your insights can be valuable to the advice seeker.

Primarily, you provide a sounding board, listening for gaps in his logic, missing information, tangent trails or dangers lurking out of sight along the paths he has proposed to take. Being a good adviser is often like being a good journalist—you listen for and investigate who, what, when, where, why, how.

In most cases, the advice seeker will have provided these answers, and your job will be to expand his answers or think of new ones that may be more suitable. Often you're like the professor who guides a graduate student in his doctoral research, asking questions that will lead the student down new paths of investigation rather than answering questions or closing doors in his face. Be careful here that you keep the other's motivation and goals foremost in your mind, not your own. Otherwise, the advice will be useless.

One word of caution: Always remember that the other person has final say about the decision. He or she has the most information and must take all the risks to put the decision into action. You can damage a relationship or put undue pressure on it by investing too much emotionally in the situation and forcing your advice upon the other person.

Above all, be aware of the dangers in giving unworkable advice. Where will you stand if things don't turn out so well?

You remember the results of Jezebel's advice to her husband Ahab about buying Naboth's vineyard (1 Kings 21). King Ahab tried to buy the vineyard, but Naboth didn't want to sell it because it had been in the family for generations. Jezebel, however, wasn't as ready to take "no" for an answer as her husband. She advised him to let her take care of the matter; whereupon, she had lying witnesses accuse Naboth of cursing God and the king, and she had him stoned. But instead of the outcome she predicted, God's prophet Elijah met King Ahab at the vineyard as he was about to possess it and pronounced God's verdict on his wife's deed. Ahab's whole family was to be cursed, including Jezebel, and their bodies were to be eaten by dogs and vultures.

Not even the most qualified professional advisers guarantee results. Trainers never promise their athletes that if they train eight hours a day, they will win an Olympic medal. Nor do stockbrokers promise their investors that if they buy certain stocks they will double their money in six months. Can you afford to be more confident in the advice you give? Guard against letting a more naive advice seeker take your advice as "gospel" and bank all he has emotionally, physically, or spiritually on your counsel.

Receiving

So how do you let people know whether you're in the market for advice? Many people constantly complain about a certain person on the job or a relative at home who continually pours out "should" and "oughts." Yet others seldom have anyone trying to tell them what to do. What makes the difference? Is it just that some families or offices have no resident advisers while others abound with people who can never keep their opinions to themselves?

For the most part, people who continually get advice, either wanted or unwanted, are those who have not learned to signal others to turn off the flow. Consider the situation with Naomi and her two daughters-in-law, Orpah and Ruth.

You'll remember that after Naomi's husband and two sons died, leaving all three women widows, Naomi decided to return to her homeland of Judah and advised her daughters-in-law to return to their own country.

Orpah took her advice; Ruth didn't. Why? Let's take a look at the passage (Ruth 1:18, TLB):

> And again they cried together, and Orpah kissed her mother-in-law good-bye, and returned to her childhood home; but Ruth insisted on staying with Naomi.
>
> "See," Naomi said to her, "your sister-in-law has gone back to her people and to her gods; you should do the same."
>
> But Ruth replied, "Don't make me leave you, for I want to go wherever you go, and to live wherever you live; your people shall be my people, and your God shall be my God; I want to die where you die, and be buried there. May the Lord do terrible things to me if I allow anything but death to separate us."
>
> And when Naomi saw that Ruth had made up her mind and could not be persuaded otherwise, she stopped urging her.

Ruth's mind was made up, we would say today. A firm resolution stopped Naomi's protest about what was best for her daughter-in-law; it still works in most situations today. People tend to give advice only when they feel that there's some chance of your listening, some chance that you're still in the market for opposing opinions.

Therefore, to curb advice that always seems to come your way, reconsider the signals you're giving. Are you conveying the fact that you are still ambivalent about decisions you've said you've already made? Do your eyes, body language, or manner of behavior undermine your words?

If you *are* giving ambiguous messages and *do* resent interference, be firm with comments like: "I have already made my decision; I'd rather not discuss it any longer. Or, "I have the information I need; I'll be making my own decision sometime next month." Finally, assure the would-be adviser that you will take responsibility for the possible consequences.

Parents, particularly, feel that they will be held responsible for their children's wrong decisions and have to pick up the pieces. It's difficult to lay aside that thought where grown children are concerned. Grown children can help by reassuring the advice giver that they are aware that things may not work out as hoped, but that they still will be able to handle the consequences of a mistake.

Don't be hasty, however, in spurning advice when the stakes are high and your direction is murky. Evidently, the writer of Proverbs considered it wise to seek advice:

Without counsel plans go wrong, but with many advisers they succeed (Prov. 15:22, RSV).

Listen to advice and accept instruction, that you may gain wisdom for the future (Prov. 19:20, RSV).

Plans are established by counsel; by wise guidance wage war (Prov. 20:18, RSV).

Don't go to war without wise guidance; there is safety in many counselors (Prov. 24:6, TLB).

But even though many people seek advice of some kind before they embark on a monumental decision, the advice they get is not always dependable. That's true not necessarily because someone gives bad advice, but rather because the seeker goes about soliciting advice in the wrong way.

Wrong Ways to Get Advice

One of the more ineffective ways of asking for advice is to set out all the facts and your tentative decision and then hint that you'd like the other person to agree with your choice. This approach is like fishing for compliments: "I shopped all day for this suit to wear to the awards dinner. It's so important to me that I look my best. It costs a fortune! Well? Do you like it?" What's a friend going to say?

The same goes for advice. The correlative is something like the following: "An acquaintance of mine at work invited my family and me to go on a ski trip next month to Aspen. But the last few days, this 'friend' and I haven't been getting along at work. In fact, I think he'd rather we back out of the trip altogether. But I've promised my kids, and I don't think it'd be fair to them to mess up their spring vacation. So I figure he invited us and we should go, unless he comes right out and withdraws the invitation. I mean, he's the one who mentioned it in the first place, and we *have* spent the money on new ski clothes. If he and his family want to change their minds about making the trip with us, they can just stay home. . . . You think I'm right in this, don't you?"

It's the same fishing expedition. You're not really asking for advice; you're stating an opinion and asking the friend to back you up.

A second mistake we often make in asking for advice is to state our opinion and then argue when the other person contradicts it. A few years ago when I was first thinking of establishing a consulting business, a would-be adviser called my hand on my claim to want his opinion:

Me: "I'm wondering if I should get an answering service or buy an answering machine."

Don: "I'd do it right from the very start—get an answering service. People don't like to talk to a machine."

Me: "But do you know how much an answering service costs?"

Don: "It's worth it to have your clients talk to a real live person, though. Somebody who can answer questions when you're out of the office."

Me: "But I really won't be out of the office that much."

Don: "Having an answering service gives the best impression, too. Those answering machines sound like some fly-by-night place. When you're selling only a service and have no product to show, you've got to be careful about your image."

Me: "But I've talked to two other people who say their machines work fine."

Don: "Consultants?"

Me: "No. Salespersons."

Don: "They have a product to sell. You're in a service."

Me: "But I can't see paying $60 a month for someone to answer maybe four or five calls."

Don: "So why did you ask me what I thought?"

Me: (Embarrassed) "I just wanted to get your opinion."

Don: "Well, that's what I gave you."

Needless to say, I changed my approach before asking the next person for advice about the business. Listen the next time you seek advice to see if you're verbally shadow-boxing with objections and alternatives rather than welcoming new ideas. Sooner or later, the other person will get the picture that you don't really want alternate ideas, not only want to play solitaire, and to cheat at that, if necessary to win!

One final ineffective approach in asking for advice is the habit of asking for opinions until you find one you like. Although Proverbs does tell us that there is safety in many advisers, there should be method to selecting the many counselors.

To turn the ineffective into the useful, let me suggest some guidelines for asking for and receiving sound advice.

Wise Ways to Get Advice

Ask the proper person(s).—That sounds obvious, but actually few people are so methodical in their quest for advice that they choose their counselors with much forethought. Many seek advice from whoever is around at the time or whoever they think likes them well enough to take the time to listen to the problem or facts. And some even go so far as to eliminate advisers solely on the chance that they may give an opinion they don't like.

Even King Ahab, who hated God's prophet Micaiah, knew it was definitely in his best interest to find the man and listen to what he had to say. First Kings 22 tells us that after his four hundred heathen prophets agreed with his plan to attack Ramoth-gilead, Ahab still had his doubts, as did King Jehoshaphat, who planned to make the attack a joint effort. Though reluctant to do so because Micaiah had the reputation for gloomy predictions, Ahab called for his advice. Sure enough, it was more of the same. Micaiah predicted defeat. But rather than listen, even though he knew that he'd finally found the "right" person in God's prophet, Ahab followed the advice of the majority, who told him what he wanted to hear. The outcome, of course, was disaster.

If we learn anything from King Ahab we learn the importance of seeking the right adviser. Specifically, that means someone who has a right relationship with God, someone who has the experience that would enable him to know about our situation, someone who is free from prejudice, someone who is not too emotionally involved to have a stake in the outcome but who cares enough to take the time to give us his best.

When you have a loved one dying of a rare disease, you seek out the doctor who specializes in its treatment—not necessarily the one closest to your house. It should be the same in seeking advice on important issues in your life. Choose counselors with care.

Ask specifically for what you need—ideas, insights, data, instruction, reactions, or personal experience.—Only you know exactly what help you need in working out a problem or reaching your decision. If you have chosen an adviser deliberately to ask about one particular situation, you should let him or her in on the "why" of your choice.

Tell him you'd like advice based on his personal experience, work expertise, access to specific data—whatever the reason you considered him to be a competent adviser. We've all heard of the dentist's children who have cavities and the plumber's wife who has to unclog her own drains. Simply because you choose a certain person from whom to get advice doesn't necessarily mean she will tell you the information you most value from her. If you want hard, cold facts, ask for facts. If you want new ideas, ask for ideas. If you want him to punch holes in your reasoning, ask for the soft spots. If you'll settle for personal experience, ask for personal experience.

Try these comments to get specifics: "Can you think of additional options that I haven't considered?" "Do you have any figures that would throw some light on my decision?" "So I've laid out my basic reasoning; can you see any gaps in my logic?" "What other consequences can you see down the road if I take course of action B?" "I know you've raised four teenagers who kept their faith all through the years, even after their marriages; did you ever have a problem in getting them to attend church? If so, how did you handle the situation?" To get specific advice, ask specific questions.

Ask for comparisons based on criteria you can understand.—For example, someone's "excellent" may be the next person's "good."

My consulting business has made me much more aware of the importance of eliminating as many of the variables as possible. At the conclusion of my writing workshops, I distribute reaction sheets for participants to rate the workshop content, leader, and learning experience, and then to answer other open-ended questions about improvements.

On one particular reaction sheet, a participant may check everything—content, leader, overall learning—as "excellent." And then at the bottom of the sheet, he or she will make three or four suggestions for improvements! "I wish we had had more time for individual assignments." "Perhaps you could supply a bibliography for further reading." "The format should be changed. I don't like working so intensely late in the afternoon."

Then on another reaction sheet, another participant will check content, leader, and overall learning "good" and under "suggestions for improvements," will respond: "Needs no improvement; everything was great." Inconsistent? Maybe and maybe not. Meanings are in people, not in words.

When you ask for advice then, you need to ask the adviser to make comparisons you can understand. Not, "Do you think Cary Martin would work well with the other ladies on this project?" But, "Do you think Cary Martin or Cheryl Glass would work better with the other ladies on this project?"

Not, "I'm in charge of the seating arrangements and refreshments and I was wondering if you expect a good attendance at the conference?" But, "I'm in charge of the seating arrangements and refreshments, and I was wondering how many you expect to attend the conference. We had about 200 last year. Do you expect more or fewer than that?"

Don't give too much detail too soon and "freeze" the adviser with information overload.—Much of the time the reason we ourselves become bogged down when making a decision is that we feel too heavily the consequences of a wrong decision.

Roger A. Golde, in his excellent book *What You Say Is What You Get*, warns that when asking for advice, we need to be careful not to "freeze" the person advising us.[1] Otherwise, every gate that he mentions, which could lead to an escape from our problem, we block by throwing out another inhibiting "fact" or detail. Pretty soon, the adviser is overcome with the weight and density of the problem too!

Stifle objections and sift through the advice for usable insights and approaches, while discarding the rest.—Mouthing his reactions too soon almost prevented Naaman's being healed of leprosy. You recall the story of his arrival at Elisha's home to ask for advice on how to cure his leprosy (2 Kings 5). Elisha sent a messenger out to tell Naaman to go to the Jordan River and dip seven times to be cured. Instead of being thrilled at the easy solution, Naaman stalked away angrily and complained to his servants: "Why the Jordan River? Aren't the Abana River and the Pharpar River just as good?" But his officers reasoned with him: "If the prophet had advised something more difficult, wouldn't you have done it?" So Naaman swallowed his objections and obeyed, receiving the healing immediately.

Often, we too may stifle the good ideas we receive from advisers because of our tendency to play devil's advocate with their suggestions. Once you call his hand on the first useless idea, an adviser soon learns to play it safe and withhold all suggestions to keep from having to defend himself. If you don't agree with his advice, you don't have to say so on the spot. Simply listen and discard it, and, if necessary, say that you'll give the suggestion more thought later. The procedure is much like preventing frozen water pipes. You turn them on and keep the water flowing, because once the water stops, it freezes hard.

Let the ideas come; you can sort and use or discard later.

Separating the Wheat from the Chaff

When discarding or retaining advice, keep in mind these guidelines.

First, your presentation of the details, to a large extent, colors the advice you get. You may subconsciously withhold details from your adviser in describing the situation, problem, or whatever and limit his view of the situation. Or you may give greater emphasis to some concerns than others, tipping the scales in a particular direction. In other words, the advice you get may be largely your own.

Also, remember that most people will do their best to tell you what they think you want to hear. That's why it's important that, as far as possible, you give the adviser "permission" to disagree with you and to tell you what might be upsetting: "I guess you can tell from the way I've described the procedure that I don't like it and don't think it'll work. But I realize I'm already prejudiced about this because it'll involve so much extra work. I hope I'm overlooking some good points that you can see. Be objective and tell me what you think about the procedure. Never mind that I might not agree."

Another thing in evaluating the advice you receive is to remember that no one adviser can see the *full* picture. Usually everyone draws her own advice from her own personal experience. Perhaps that's why Solomon in his Proverbs commented on the safety in a multitude of advisers. Remember that when someone tells you something won't work or isn't a good idea, he's speaking from one person's perspective. Take his advice for what one opinion is worth; then confirm or reject it by asking others for their experience also.

Remember, too, that personal philosophy dictates the advice others give. Rehoboam, at his inauguration after King Solomon's death, requested advice from two groups of men but gave little thought to the personal philosophy that accompanied each group's counsel (1 Kings 12). When his subjects came to Rehoboam with their concern that he not treat them as badly as had his father

Solomon, they demanded his "philosophy" for ruling them before they would pledge their allegiance to him.

Rehoboam asked for three days to think over his answer, and then sought advice: The older statesmen of the country, having seen how Solomon's rough treatment and heavy taxation had taken toll on lives and loyalty, advised Rehoboam to rule with a hand of kindness. But Rehoboam then turned to his young friends with whom he'd grown up and asked their opinion. "Be a hard taskmaster and show them who's king!" they advised. Again, personal philosophy.

Very little advice of importance can be separated from one's *weltanschauung*, or "world view." You remember the advice from Job's friends. Their personal philosophy led them to lengthy expositions: "You're suffering, Job, because of your sin; you need to confess."

One's *weltanschauung* may encompass any number of "truths," such as: "It is more blessed to give than receive"; "Man is innately good (or evil)"; "There is no heaven (or hell)"; "Live for today." Whatever "truths" make up a person's view of himself, his fellow-man, and God color his perception of most situations and flavor the advice he gives.

That means that the ultimate decision or action must be yours, because no one will assign the same values to each item on the scorecard as you would.

To illustrate, let's say a Bible teacher has been working for over a year to get Aileen to attend a study session and that finally she promises to attend the following Thursday evening. But before the Thursday meeting, the teacher develops a sore throat and her husband advises her to cancel the Thursday meeting. Obviously, the husband assigns greater value to his wife's health than to Aileen's attendance; therefore, the choice is obvious—to cancel.

The Bible teacher, however, may decide to go ahead and lead the Bible study, because she assigns greater value to the fact that Aileen will be present than she does to her own comfort.

Of course, this is a simplified evaluation, more or less representative of the kind we face every day. But the same principle holds no matter what the values involved. For example, which weighs more in the decision of a family doctor: convenience of location or office-visit charge? Which weighs more in the decision of a job change: possibility for promotion or security? Which weighs more in deciding on church membership: the pastor's sermons or the youth program? It depends on who's doing the weighing.

So, when asking for advice, don't expect the adviser to be able to give you the final tally on all the issues involved; he or she can only help you *view* the items, not *score* them.

Above all, in asking for and receiving advice, don't take the adviser for granted. Say "thank you." Anytime someone advises you, he or she has invested time and emotional energy in the situation. Sometimes advisors actually invest so much that they become annoyed when you don't follow their solutions. On the other hand, some who receive advice either directly or indirectly become angry when the advice doesn't work out well. To avoid hard feelings on either end of the spectrum—receiver or giver—let the process end with the advice given, not the action or inaction that follows.

The next time you're tempted to say, "If I were you, I'd . . . " do a little more mind reading. Ask yourself if the other person *really* wants your opinion or rather wants encouragement with his own. If you're certain that she really has singled you out for advice, play your role by acting as a stimulant, pointing out possible alternatives, fresh ideas, facts, personal experience—all labeled specifically as such. Leave the actual decision in the other person's hands, no matter how tempted you are to play fortune-teller.

And when unsolicited advice finds its path to your door, you can minimize feelings of rejection for the giver if you firmly explain that you are no longer in the market for suggestions—anybody's suggestions. And for those times when you *do* need helpful advice, ask the proper person for a specific perspective based on criteria you understand. Then stifle it—that is, stifle your temptation to keep interfering and refuting his reasoning.

Go with the flow; dam up the water you can use, and let the rest rush on downstream.

5

"I don't mean to be critical, but. . . "

Giving and Receiving Criticism

Why is "constructive" criticism almost always destructive? Consider the last time someone told you something "for your own good." Has your teenager mentioned that you'd look ten years younger if you took off about twenty pounds? Has a neighbor confided that maybe your yard could use a little more fertilizer to look as green as his? Has your Bible study teacher complained that you need to put more emphasis on reaching out to the lost rather than socializing among yourselves? What was your reaction to your spouse's comment that your solo had a "nasal" quality?

Constructive or destructive? What matters is how the criticized person feels, not what the criticizer's intentions may be, however noble. Furthermore, most criticism focuses on the past and makes the receiver feel that nothing can be done to alter the "error," other than to grin and bear it.

That is not to say that there is never an occasion for criticism, but rather that we should be aware of the effects of even our well-intentioned remarks.

We can learn much, however, from a study of how Jesus used criticism, with full knowledge of what effect it had on the receiver. You recall his manner, recorded in John 8, when he intervenes on the mob action as the people surround the adulterous woman. Although aware that the scribes and Pharisees were attempting to trap him in a question about obedience to Moses' law, Jesus, even when alone with the woman, refused to criticize her actions. Instead, he concentrated on instruction for the future: "Neither do I condemn thee: go, and sin no more."

But Jesus did use criticism from time to time when his intentions were to strip others of their pride and bring them to repentance. He often referred to the spiritually proud as a "generation of vipers" and the "stiffnecked." Yet even when our intention is to condemn, we must be careful about slinging critical remarks because, unlike Jesus with his divine wisdom, we cannot always assess the condition of another's heart and mind and know what he needs to prick his conscience and effect a change.

So how do you decide when to criticize others and when it is best to keep your observations to yourself? The following checklist perhaps will help you discover the effect of your remarks as well as lead to self-discovery about your own intentions, methods, and alternatives:

Do you have a "red-pencil mentality"—an attitude that searches for error?—This term used by Sidney Simon in *Negative Criticism* refers to what some seem to perceive as their mission on earth, and the church in particular—to boldly point out errors for all the world to see.[1] Upon reading the church newsletter, they forget the printed time of the budget meeting, but remember to call up the typist to "let her know" she misspelled *accommodate*. When a guest speaker occupies the pulpit, these red-pencil people don't note his exact sermon text, but rather point out to the family on the way home that his tie didn't go with his suit.

Paul, in Romans 14, spoke of this critical attitude toward weaker brothers. The attitude often becomes a compulsion, like a housewife who can't pass a picture frame without straightening it. Before you're tempted to red-pencil somebody, try to recall the sense of pride with which you turned in an English composition that had been typed with perfectly even margins and appropriate commas. Do you remember the embarrassment when the teacher passed your graded paper down the row for all to see your errors cast in red ink? Why do that to someone else? Is it really a major issue? As far as most situations go, school's out.

Am I just condemning or really guiding?—The Greek word *kritikos*, from which we get our word *criticize*, refers to the ability to discern or judge. Of all "professional critics," book or art reviewers probably adhere to this definition more closely than most. They are expected to point out the strengths and the weaknesses of a book, play, movie, or painting and to make judgments based on the evidence. Their goals are to guide readers, moviegoers, or art buyers to make appropriate choices, to influence and direct others' concepts about the work, and even to motivate the author or painter, whose work is being judged, to rise to greater accomplishments.

When you experience the urge to make judgments about another's behavior, ask yourself if you've assessed both the good and the bad, and if you intend your comments to motivate and guide future actions or merely to condemn past behavior.

Will the criticism improve the person's mental outlook and your relationship?—Will he be uplifted that you took the time to notice his action, behavior, performance, or words, and have expressed an interest in helping him improve? Is she the kind of person who will strive to make improvements, or will she feel depressed, doubt her abilities, and want to give up the effort? Will she feel more comfortable in coming to you in the future to ask for help and feedback about her improvements? Or will she be wary of your intentions and doubt that you have her best interests at heart? Will she become self-conscious around you and think that you are evaluating everything she does and keeping score? If one of these latter reactions is what you expect, perhaps you should leave the criticism to someone who has the person's fullest confidence and commitment.

How many times has this person probably heard this particular criticism before and still not made changes?—Consider why your comments would bring improvement where others have failed. Do you have more authority? More insight? More motivational information or rewards to share? If not, your comments will probably only add coals of regret and/or guilt to the fire of failure.

What are your own perceptional hangups that may be fostering inaccurate judgments?—In Matthew 7:1-5, Jesus cautioned about overlooking the log in one's own eye, while straining at the speck of imperfection in someone else's life.

Perhaps as a public-school teacher, someone has extensive experience in the principles of education. Most likely that person will expect too much from the average Bible study leader. One's expectations of that teacher's abilities may be much higher than those of other laymen who sit in the class. Likewise, jealousy or insecurity on the part of a husband may cause him to overreact when his wife gives what others would consider normal attention to friends of the opposite sex. Guard against glancing at people and situations through gray-tinted glasses that may fog your perceptions.

Could praise be just as effective as criticism in bringing about a change?—Many people have a frugal praise attitude, arguing that others "should" do what is right and expected without having to have someone pat them on the back for the effort. True. But praise has a powerful effect for making the "right" seem more attractive, workable, and worthwhile. People are generally more motivated to "improve" something good than to "redo" something bad.

For example, tell the study team of the publicity committee that you *like* their overall plan for media coverage and suggest that they *improve* it by developing two or three campaign slogans. They will work harder and perhaps even spend more time on the improvement of "something you liked," than on something you called "unfocused" or "unworkable."

Again, the apostle Paul knew the value of praise when he wrote to various congregations, complimenting them on their generosity in offerings, hospitality to fellow travelers, and faithfulness in prayer. And Jesus did not condemn Thomas, who refused to believe in his resurrection unless he could place his hand in his Savior's side. He used praise to encourage others' belief in things to come: "Thomas, because thou hast seen me, thou hast believed: blessed are they that have not seen, and yet have believed" (John 20:29).

Consider the criticism you have in mind to see how it might be turned into a plus rather than a minus beside the individual's behavior.

Could you use a problem-solving technique, rather than criticism, to bring about change?—As a student teacher, my confidence and enthusiasm waned during the course of my first eighth-grade English class. Although the students were eager to make me look good while my university supervisor sat in the back of the room critiquing my performance, their answers did not always follow the paths I had planned. But rather than provide me with a list of "thou didst wrongs" at the conclusion of the class period, the professor used three problem-solving questions to lead me to critique my own performance and solve my own problems:

"How did you think it went?" That was easy enough to answer. I immediately pointed out what I considered the bad—where I had failed to give adequate instruction and where I had expected too much of the students. But also I was quick to point out the positive that ticked along just as I'd anticipated. Next, he asked, "If you taught this class over again, what changes would you make?" Again, I suggested some alternatives to the way I'd explained a topical outline on the chalkboard and mentioned that I should have given them an easier subject to try outlining. Finally, he concluded our session with, "What help, resources, or information would you like to have from me or your partner teacher?" Again, I was eager to find out if the school system kept old grammar texts in storage from which I could gather some additional samples for quizzes. Also, I asked about a catalog of library films available from the university's education department.

And that was the end of a helpful, problem-solving critique. I had no further apprehension about his next unscheduled visits to my classroom. If he happened to appear on a "bad" day, I assumed the critiquing session would turn into one of problem solving.

Jesus, of course, was master of meeting people's needs by offering alternatives rather than criticism. To the Samaritan woman at the well, he offered living water that would quench her thirst for a fulfilling relationship, rather than condemning her for her past marital record.

When prone to criticize, put your mind into a problem-solving mode and see if the results aren't more appropriate.

Even after passing your criticisms and thoughts through all of these filters, you may *still* feel that you should offer your comments. Perhaps you have a close, loving relationship with someone and feel the Holy Spirit's leadership to pass on judgments, much as the book reviewer does, to build the person up and to inspire him to greater things. In that case, *how* becomes the question.

In writing to the Corinthians, Paul knew the dangers of expressing his helpful remarks in the wrong way: "Therefore I write these things being absent, lest being present I should use sharpness, according to the power which the Lord hath given me to edification, and not to destruction" (2 Cor. 13:10). He knew that God was directing him to offer criticisms for the purpose of building them up, but he wasn't too confident of his own ability to express his thoughts so that they'd have the intended good results.

Most of us have the same anxiety—or should have—when we express something that could be taken as criticism. The following guidelines should help you turn your critique of someone's behavior, words, or attitude into edifying, rather than devastating, remarks:

Criticism—Do I Dare and How Do I Dare?

(1) Understand the situation before you give the answer: Some people shoot out criticism as it rolls through their minds, leaving the hearer to sort out what's applicable and what's not. Such a habit leads to one of two results: either the hearer learns to tune out everything that's said, or he becomes so discouraged that he gives up trying to please. As a guard against this assembly-line approach, make sure you have the facts and thoroughly understand the behavior before you form opinions about what went wrong and what should have happened.

As a writing consultant myself, I know from experience that consultants who walk in with all the answers walk out very fast. Clients must explain their situations, problems, and needs before they can trust that the consultant's answers are the right ones. As soon as someone learns that you don't have all the facts—only the answers—your well-meaning comments to a friend about how he disciplines his children fall on deaf ears.

(2) Separate fact from opinion. I recently overheard these comments about a preacher: "He simply doesn't prepare. It's the same sermon over and over every Sunday. He starts with a different text, but five minutes into the thing, he's back to the same old one, two,

three." On the whole, these comments sound like fact, but are they? Has the observer checked to see how much time has actually been spent in preparation? Has he kept track of the sermon points and illustrations, and does he have dates on which they were repeated? Although his comments may *seem* like fact, others in the congregation would probably disagree, insisting that every time he uses a certain anecdote it's to illustrate a different point. Or, what's more common, they may not even recall ever having heard the illustration the criticizer says has been worn out from overuse.

A case in point: A few years ago when our pastor resigned, the church decided to give him a congenial "roast" as part of his farewell banquet. As one of the four speakers, I chose to weave my remarks around the fact that this pastor has an excellent memory. After comments about how he could remember everyone's children's, grandchildren's, and great-grandchildren's birthdays and anniversaries, I proceeded to say that he had only one fault with memory—he couldn't remember that he'd told the same jokes over and over. His wife and I had earlier put our heads together to come up with a list of his favorites. At the roast, I intended to illustrate my point by starting one of his old jokes, and then to have the audience as a group call out the punch line. It worked beautifully as the group chorused each punch line—except for the last joke I began; no one in the audience acted as if they'd ever heard it. And in my faulty perception and memory, he'd told the joke from the pulpit at least a hundred times. And to think, no one but his wife and I remembered it!

Watch such opinions of yours passed off as facts. Rather than say, "He can't sing," say "I don't think he sings well," or "He seems to have trouble with the high notes." Rather than say, "She's wishy-washy," give the facts: "She has reversed her previous recommendation several times."

(3) Criticize yourself first and assume some of the blame. Perhaps this is why the editorial "we" has come into use. Speakers, above all, appreciate the difference in audience reception in the following two statements: "Our church hasn't grown in the past two years as it should have. Perhaps I haven't had my priorities in the correct order

and haven't spent enough time in leading you to reach out." As opposed to: "This church hasn't grown in the past two years as it should have. You don't have your priorities in the correct order, and you don't spend enough time reaching out."

Most mature adults realize that conflicts are rarely one-sided; and even when this is not the case and you're not involved, be willing to shoulder some of the blame simply because you have the ego strength to do so. It will make the other's burden lighter.

(4) Don't analyze why someone does or feels a certain way: "I think you simply refuse to be on time when we're supposed to go somewhere for dinner because you know it irritates me," says a husband to his wife as they leave the house. "It gives you a real sense of power, doesn't it? I have people doing what I say when I say all day long and then I come home and you can manage to break the routine. You do it because you saw your mother do the same thing to your dad and embarrass him."

Forget assumptions about someone else's motivation. Never assume someone has behaved badly or botched a job on purpose. Perhaps he lacks maturity, knowledge, or skills. Analyzing only serves to humiliate, embarrass, anger, or all three. The reasons and motivations may seem plausible to you, but it is best to leave the psychiatry to the professionals.

(5) Include some credits with your criticisms. How many times have you said to a depressed family member or friend, "Nothing can be all bad." Yet when in the emotional throes of disgust over someone's behavior, our words seem to refute the idea, refusing to acknowledge even the slightest good. Paul, in his famous address to the Athenians on Mars Hill, began by giving credit to his listeners for the fact that they were very meticulous in their worship, even so far as to constructing an altar to the unknown god. Then he proceeded to add to their knowledge, telling them about the one true God.

To give credits along with criticisms not only encourages your listener, but also adds weight to your criticism. If the listener admires your good sense in recognizing his strengths, he will also sense your attempt to be objective about his weaknesses.

But be careful when you're sandwiching criticism between credits that you use "and" statements, rather than "but" statements.
Not:
"I appreciate your prayers, but we also need your financial support."
Rather:
"I appreciate your prayers, and we also need your financial support."

Not:
"Thank you for calling, but I really don't feel like talking now."
Rather:
"Thank you for calling, and I'll really feel more like talking in a couple of days."

Not:
"The teachers have been careful to pick up the trash on Sunday mornings, but on Sunday nights things have been left in a mess."
Rather:
"The teachers have been careful to pick up the trash on Sunday mornings, and Sunday night is the problem now—things have been left in a mess."

"But" statements tend to cancel out the credit you've just given beforehand. Mary Poppins was right; a spoonful of sugar makes the medicine go down—sometimes.

(6) Don't get personal; criticize only the viewpoint or behavior. Recall Jesus' comments to Peter when he foretold his denial. He stated the facts about Peter's behavior: "Verily I say unto thee, That this night, before the cock crow, thou shalt deny me thrice" (Matt. 26:34). He did *not* say, "You're weak and fickle, Peter." In talking to the Samaritan woman at the well, he stated that she had had five husbands, *not* "You've got to learn to control your lust, lady; you just don't know how to build a true loving relationship." When intervening in the family dispute between Mary and Martha, he simply stated the facts about Martha's concern. "Martha, thou art careful and troubled about many things. But one thing is needful" (Luke 10:41-42). Notice that he failed to draw conclusions about her personhood and left comments like, "Martha, you're a nag," unsaid.

(7) Use phrases that build, not destroy, goodwill: You've heard it

said that it's not what you say, but how you say it. That could never be more true than when leveling criticism at someone. Consider the difference in your responses to these versions of the same sentiment:

"This should teach you a lesson."
   versus
"This has really caused some problems, hasn't it?"

"Let me tell you something, Son."
   versus
"We need to discuss something, Son."

"You're doing it the slowest possible way."
   versus
"I've got an idea for a faster way to do that."

"I don't need your help."
   versus
"I'll certainly consider any suggestions you have."

"Why did you decide to do such a stupid thing?"
   versus
"There must be some reason that you decided to do that."

(8) Be specific, not general. Specific criticisms, more than general ones, help the hearer understand and correct the behavior. When the rich young ruler came to Jesus and asked what he needed to do to inherit eternal life, Jesus didn't give him a platitude like, "Change your priorities." Instead, he translated his need for personal and complete commitment to a specific action that would illustrate a changed heart: "Sell all that thou hast, and distribute unto the poor" (Luke 18:22).

"You're inconsiderate" leaves a lot of room for interpretation. Better to say, "Next time, asking others where they'd like to eat lunch would be more considerate." You may know what you mean by "ineffective procedures," "selfish motives," "mission minded," or "church policy," but don't assume that your hearer does.

(9) Avoid the "halo" and "pitchfork" tendency. That is, avoid the tendency to focus on one good or bad trait or behavior and let that overshadow your opinion about everything else. We see this "halo"

effect frequently with regard to celebrities who become well known for one accomplishment or skill and then try their hand at everything. Someone who's a great comic begins to get offers from everywhere to act, sing, dance, or sell soap—none of which he may have the talent to do.

This tendency has also been substantiated by psychologists in study after study, particularly in the field of education. Once teachers "peg" certain students about their abilities—he's either an "A" student or a "C" student—they tend to give the same grades throughout the year. When eraser marks are found on the wall, Johnny Troublemaker is the first to be blamed, often without even examining the evidence. Sometimes contest judges make special effort to guard against this "halo" or "pitchfork" phenomenon by insisting that all people make their entries anonymously to ensure objectivity.

Jesus, of course, gave us the ultimate example in digging beneath the unflattering surface and spotting the redeeming qualities in people such as Mary Magdalene. We should guard against the faulty reasoning expressed in this statement: "She taught in both the preschool and children's divisions and never could relate to the kids. I just don't think we should hire her as organist."

(10) Never say *never, always, totally, completely.* "You never tell me when you're going to be late for dinner," generally brings the response, "Yes, I do. I called you last Monday to tell you I was going to stop by the ball field that night." The hearer focuses on the absolute word in your statement and immediately supplies the evidence to shoot holes in your blanket condemnation. But, of course, you come back with, "Well, I didn't mean 'always'; 99 percent of the time you do." Then you start over where the hearer should have come in the first time. Criticisms that begin with absolutes usually revolve around exceptions and seldom get the desired results in changing the habitual viewpoint or behavior.

(11) Criticize one thing at a time. More overpowers and discourages. Changes in behavior aren't made overnight. In police vernacular, when you "throw the book at someone," he'll likely close it without making any changes. Consider the reaction you get from your kids on Saturday morning when you announce housecleaning

chores: "I need some help and I want you to do the breakfast dishes, dust, clean the bathrooms, vacuum, and sweep the patio." I don't know about you, but I get better results when I assign one task to one child at one time. The same goes for criticism; ask for one change in behavior at a time.

(12) Criticize to some end, and offer your help with the resolution. One of the prominent characteristics of destructive criticism is that it only applies to the past. To be helpful, turn your comments into a challenge for the future—a mutual goal, if possible: "So you see, the orphanage ministry is receiving most of the money. What we need to work toward is a better system for disbursements, one into which the whole group has input. I have a couple of suggestions for such a system and maybe you do, too."

Back to Paul's sermon on Mars Hill. After pointing out the Athenians' ignorance in worshiping false, powerless gods, he directed them to an alternative, worshiping the one true God. Jesus dealt with Peter, James, and John in the same manner. Taking them into the garden of Gethsemane, he asked them to remain behind and pray; but upon returning, he found them sleeping. His rebuke was to some effect—with purpose and a common goal: "Simon, sleepest thou? couldest not thou watch one hour? Watch ye and pray, lest ye enter into temptation" (Mark 14:37-38). However, when Jesus returned to the disciples the third time and again found them asleep, his comments were quite different: "Sleep on now, and take your rest: it is enough, the hour is come" (v. 41). In other words, when the reason for their praying was over, he saw no need to criticize them again; no purpose to the rebuke. Instead, he offered understanding.

Be willing to help those you criticize see a purpose and find a solution to what you are criticizing. Don't simply berate their negligence.

(13) Don't belabor the point. A few months ago, I had occasion to welcome a new teacher to our staff. Knowing that she had quit teaching jobs several times over the years out of frustration about keeping control in the classroom, I wanted to make sure that she started out on solid footing. Scheduling a private consultation before the regular staff meeting, I repeated at length all the cautions I

could think of about control, discipline, rapport, preparation, confidence. When I finally wound down and gave her a chance to respond, she faced me with a sardonic twinkle in her eye, "I think I've got the point." She made hers; I shut up.

Parents, you, too, may have noticed this tendency in yourself when, after a long bit of "correction," your child's exasperation comes to the point that he explodes with "OK, OK, OK, I hear you." Translated that means, "You told me already, and already, and already."

Possibly God called Nathan to be his prophet because he could make few words so memorable. After David had committed adultery with Bathsheba and had caused her husband's death, Nathan came to him with a story about a rich man who owned many sheep and had stolen from a poor man with only one lamb that he loved as a pet. After his story had made the point about the greed and injustice of the rich man, Nathan said simply to David: "Thou art the man" (2 Sam. 12:7). In the verses to follow, as Nathan delivers God's judgments, he does not have to convince David any further of his guilt.

The same is true in most situations. Others are acutely aware of their weaknesses; what they need is someone with solutions and challenges to improvement. Enough said?

(14) Is the time right? Jesus promised that he would not permit our burden of temptation to become more than we could bear, but would make a way of escape. Unfortunately, we do not always do likewise when criticizing our fellowmen. Before you pronounce your judgments, make sure you know what the individual's other concerns and problems are at the present—at home, work, school, church. Are you sure that this comment of yours won't be the proverbial straw that breaks the camel's back? Sometimes we are fooled by an outer facade of strength, when the person may be near to crumbling on the inside.

Paul showed particular sensitivity about timing when he wrote his many letters to the various churches, stating that he had other things to say, but that he wanted to wait until he could be there in person. Evidently, he felt that some were not strong enough spiritually to understand or to accept his criticisms and make a change without his personal help. Sensitivity to time and place is never more important than when criticizing.

(15) Don't criticize the guilty and the innocent alike in a group setting. The innocent resent your remarks, and the guilty figure everybody else must have been doing the same thing and excuse themselves. When Jesus gathered his disciples in the upper room the night of his betrayal, he did not harangue the group about their upcoming disloyalty. Rather, he served them and washed their feet—all twelve. Only one, he warned, would betray him that night. He had no indictment for the whole group. (His sermons and teachings, of course, fall into another category of instruction rather than criticism.)

Yet time and again church leaders and family heads make the mistake of group critique or punishment both of which only lead to resentment from the majority.

The same principle applies in the classroom. A teacher knows that group correction is not nearly as effective as an individual talk after class. And group punishment does little but build resentment among the innocent. Likewise, a group critique on family vacation such as, "You two kids need to quiet down in the backseat," usually brings two responses: From the innocent, "I wasn't being loud." From the guilty, "OK"—with little change in behavior since he was not specifically singled out.

Reactions—Do I Take This Lying Down?

So much for giving criticism. Although many criticizers begin their comments with "I hate to say this, but, . . . " most of us don't hate giving criticism nearly as much as receiving it. And that reaction goes to underscore my earlier point—that constructive criticism is most often destructive. The receiver's reaction, not the giver's intentions, determines the good or bad that usually comes from the critical remarks.

So, how do most people respond when they're criticized?

The first, almost automatic reaction to criticism is to deny its validity. Usually the comeback is an outright, "That's not true." Or, perhaps it begins, "Yes, but, . . . " followed by excuses or reasons the evidence can't be taken at face value. When someone criticizes our ideas, there is the tendency to marshall forces and argue our own position more forcefully instead of holding our ideas up to the light for closer scrutiny. Those who listened to Jesus' teachings about marriage and divorce reacted the same way to his comments that God intended marriage to last a lifetime (Matt. 19:6-7). The Pharisees came back with "Why then, . . . " reminding him that Moses had commanded that they draw up a bill of divorcement. Arguing our own points often closes our minds to the validity of another's perceptions.

And not only do we react "yes, but, . . . " when our *ideas* are criticized. Often, our reaction comes from a sense of wounded pride, an attempt to defend our image. "Yes, my decision did violate church policy on that matter, but I had no way of knowing that the policy was still being enforced." Translated, that means, "I'm not the kind of person who would do anything underhanded. Did you think I was?"

It's to your advantage to squelch the almost instantaneous reaction to deny and to take time to examine what has been said. Perhaps you need to stall for time to make the appropriate examination: "I haven't considered my views (or behavior) in that light; I'd like to have some time to think over what you said. May I phone you later today?"

A second common reaction to criticism, both justified and un-justified, is to counterattack. "Well, sure, I took it upon myself to make that decision without consulting you, because you never come to the committee meetings anyway." Or, "Why should I stay home every night, when all you ever do is watch TV when I'm around?" You can rest assured that most of the discussion to follow these counterattacks will center on personal shortcomings and the real issues about the lack of communication will get little wear and tear because they won't surface too often. Even if the accuser has faults that you think contribute to your criticized behavior, it is more effective to listen to the other's perception of the problem with an open mind. Admit your shortcomings and express interest in finding a solution. And *then* explain how you think the other's behavior contributes to your problem, or better, could contribute to the solution.

Take the preceding example. How much more effective could the discussion have been with a response like the following: "Yes, I did make that decision without consulting you, and I shouldn't have. Sometimes it just doesn't seem expedient to phone all the committee members before responding to something I consider minor. Maybe you could suggest a time when our committee could meet so that you could be sure to be able to attend?"

Or, about the husband-wife situation: "You're right about my schedule—at least this week, for sure. I have been gone four nights and that's too much. But I feel that when I'm home, we don't get to spend much time together anyway. If I stayed home more often, would you be willing to watch less TV so that we could really talk?"

A third common reaction to criticism is an emotional collapse: humiliation, embarrassment, tears, depression, resignation. This reaction generally comes from people who have trouble separating ego from performance. When someone comments to Cheryl that she has mud on her shoe, she takes it to mean that she is a sloppy dresser. We've all known people like that. Being able to separate behavior from personal worth seems to be more difficult for some people than others. Someone who has participated in sports throughout her school years usually gets used to a coach yelling from the sidelines about a botched play, and then telling a newspaper reporter the next day she's the best player on the team. Another adult, who was berated as a child and told he would never amount to anything because he forgot to carry out the garbage, may grow up measuring his self-worth by the tasks he is or is not able to perform. To keep from letting criticism immobilize you, remember that Jesus always judged a person by what he could *become*, not by what he had done or had been.

A fourth reaction to criticism is to calmly accept all that is said as "absolute truth." We have a tendency to apply the same passivity to medicine and exercise. If it tastes bad or hurts, it must be effective. Although we may maturely "take it like a man," the criticism may be inaccurate altogether and hinder our forward progress if we put too much stock in the judgment.

Derek Johnson tells how this principle of passive acceptance applies to elephants. Trainers put heavy shackles around the foot of a baby elephant and then drive a stake in the ground to keep him from moving about very far. Of course as the elephant grows larger, he can easily break the chain and wander off, but he doesn't. Because an elephant has such a good memory, he feels the shackle around his full-grown leg and remembers his past: *I never could, so I could never.* The principle of passive acceptance is quite useful to keep huge circus animals in their places on the fair grounds while trainers put their attention elsewhere. But people should avoid falling into the same trap of accepting criticism and concluding: *I never could, so I could never. I may as well give up.* Nothing but stymied growth can follow that reaction.

Evaluations—Could the Criticizer be Right?

Instead of denial, counterattack, emotional collapse, or total acceptance, try to evaluate criticism objectively. Either learn from it or discard it. Proverbs 25:12 says, "It is a badge of honor to accept valid criticism" (TLB). The key word here is *valid,* and there are several steps you can follow to examine the validity of criticism.

The apostle Paul presents perhaps one of the best models in his response to the scathing criticism from the Corinthian Christians (2 Cor. 10—13).

First, he assessed the sources of the criticism and examined the criticizer's motives. He correctly pinpointed the instigators of all the dissatisfaction and comments leveled against him—the wolf-in-sheep's-clothing preachers who preached a different gospel from the gospel of Jesus Christ and who intended to realize some financial gain from their preaching. The more these men could discredit Paul and his message in the eyes of the Corinthian Christians, the better chance they had to gain the people's following.

Second, Paul gauged the emotional climate of the situation. Were these people sensitive to the leadership of the Holy Spirit in expressing doubts divinely placed in their hearts? Paul concluded that definitely was not the case. He knew them to be gullible, immature in their faith. And, of course, they couldn't be criticizing him at the instigation of the Holy Spirit, because they were too far away in sin—quarreling, envying, gossiping, backbiting, lustful, and immoral in other ways. In such an emotional climate, Paul decided, it was no wonder they had thrown a few darts at him, too.

Third, Paul continually reevaluated his own perceptions of himself and sought to substantiate their claims in light of others' opinions. Throughout his long letter, we hear him continually reexamining his own motives; "Why am I boasting like this?" He concluded that he was not boasting of his *own* authority, because he was a weak person who had no authority except that granted by Jesus Christ. He reaffirmed in his own mind that his reprimands came out of love for the Christians there, and not a desire to berate them and build himself up. He knew his own heart to be fearful that the believers would be led away from their devotion to the Lord just as Eve had been deceived by Satan. But wise as he was, Paul validated his self-perception by honest, open questioning about the effect he had on other churches. Did they, too, think him a fraud and a liar? Of course not. His memories (1 Thess. 3:13) of the love other churches had for him, particularly the Macedonian church, sustained him and reaffirmed his message, method, and manner in preaching the gospel.

Fourth, Paul reacted to the criticism only in so far as it applied to his goals. He constantly reminded the Christians in Corinth that his goal was their spiritual safe-keeping and maturity. He mentioned his credentials, his sufferings for Jesus' sake, and God's special revelations to him, only because it was necessary to reestablish his authority for leading them. Because his goal was not to make them see that he was a physically captivating person or a great orator, he did not defend or address the criticism leveled at his preaching or his weak physical appearance. Instead, he kept the focus of his reply on the message he preached—purity and salvation through Jesus Christ. What they thought of him personally was beside the point.

Fifth, Paul learned what he could from the criticism and discarded the rest. He particularly realized his mistake in preaching to the Corinthians free of charge—that is, letting the other churches pay for his necessities so that he would not be a burden on these baby Christians. Rather than having the effect that Paul had hoped, his actions had made his gospel and his ministry among them seem cheap. He asked forgiveness for this mistake in judgment on his part. And, as far as we know, he didn't make the same mistake again.

Finally, Paul channeled his emotional upset and energy generated by the sharp criticism into correcting the problem. In addition to writing a long, long letter to set the record straight, he decided it was time he spent a little energy on a visit to clear up the situation in Corinth.

You, too, can handle criticism in the same manner as Paul did. Instead of a denial, counterattack, emotional collapse, or total acceptance of the criticism as fact, evaluate:

Consider the source. What are the motives of your critics? Are they trying to hurt or help you? Do they stand to gain anything by putting you down? What are their credentials for making this judgment against you—what insights or special knowledge do they have that could help them see your blind spots?

Gauge the emotional climate.—Has this particular criticism been said out of rational consideration or in a moment of emotional fervor? Has the person reached this conclusion after weeks of calm observation or after only hours of upset? Is this a spirit-filled person in whose judgment I can trust, or is he speaking "in the flesh"?

Compare notes.—Have other people tried to point out to you the same faults? Work friends? Relatives? Church members? Have you yourself felt inner conflict over the same issues on previous occasions? Remember that there is wisdom in many opinions.

React to the criticism as it applies to your goals.—If someone comments that you are not a very good speaker, this may be worth your consideration and effort to correct only if you plan to make a career in sales or public speaking. If, on the other hand, someone criticizes the way you discipline your children, you need to give attention to meet your goal of becoming a wise and capable parent as the Bible instructs. If you hope to be a patient person, listen to your critic's suggestions for developing patience. Find out specifically where you've shown impatience and reassess your behavior. If someone insists that you don't keep your closets clean enough, and you're not up for Homemaker of the Year, why worry?

Learn from your mistakes and discard the unusable.—Has your critic suggested a better way to lead a class discussion so that all participants feel accepted? How can you better manage your time so that you won't neglect your family? What is it about your manner that makes your husband recoil when you try to share honest feelings? On the other hand, when others' criticisms have been evaluated in light of the previous guidelines and found invalid, discard them and move ahead with your life.

Channel the emotional upset any criticism may cause into energy to make improvements.—Is there a book that you can read to help you learn better to control your temper? Is there a more experienced parent you can spend some time with to get help with disciplining your child? Can you volunteer to be a big brother to some needy child so that you can overcome your prejudice against the poor? Can you organize a church sports league to help you learn to develop a sense of team spirit and cooperation?

The next time someone says to you, "I don't mean to be critical, but . . . , " listen and learn.

If, on the other hand, you're the one making the statement, remember that criticism should be for building up, not tearing down, an assessment of strengths as well as weaknesses. Give careful thought to your method and expression, so that the criticized will thank you for your help rather than cringe from your indictment.

"Finally, brethren, whatsoever things are true, whatsoever things are honest, whatsoever things are just, whatsoever things are pure, whatsoever things are lovely, whatsoever things are of good report; if there be any virtue, and if there be any praise, think on these things" (Phil. 4:8).

6

"I love them both, but . . . "

Peacemaking

Nothing can prove quite so uncomfortable as handling and pruning a relationship between two friends or acquaintances who have difficulties getting along. Thorns prick your good intentions and actions on every turn of the stem of that relationship until you're often tempted to let the two grow into a tangled nightmare, weeds and all.

But many of these thorny problems can be nipped in the bud by wary and capable peacemakers who hear the beginning of a problem in their presence. Not everybody is willing to get into the flower garden, however. When we hear news stories of bystanders ignoring a crime victim's cry for help, we wonder how people can be so callous and uncaring. But when relationships break around us, isn't our refusal to attempt peacemaking similar to that uncaring attitude?

The Beatitude says "Blessed are the peacemakers"; in other words, happy are the people who keep peace between themselves and others and help others reconcile their differences.

If that hasn't been your experience and if you have had bad experiences when you tried to get two people to see eye to eye, chances are that you didn't go about the peacemaking in exactly the right way.

The most successful attempts, of course, are those by which you can head off a disagreement before it permanently damages a relationship. When two people begin to express their own ideas passionately and to denigrate opposing views, try to point out that perhaps there's a misunderstanding rather than a downright disagreement. This is often the case.

Gordon: "Well, I, for one, don't want to change the church's name to Forest Corner. We've operated very well under the name we have for the last nine years and I don't see that the name Forest Corner is going to create any magic atmosphere that will have people flocking to us."

Cynthia: "But you're ignoring the fact that we haven't been growing or attracting any new members the last few years either. A name change lets people know we've started on a new course. Even in the Bible, we have records of people changing their names or God changing their names when their nature changed—like Saul to Paul, Abram to Abraham, Jacob to Israel. A name change for the church would signify a new atmosphere."

Gordon: "But what's new about another church named by location? Everything in this part of the city is "Forest Corner" something or another. I think that change just for the sake of change is silly."

Enter You: "Maybe we need to back up and clarify the basic points. Gordon, I don't think Cynthia was necessarily saying that we should change the name to Forest Corner, but rather simply that she'd like to see a name change to reflect a change in the church's nature and direction. Did I understand you correctly?"

Cynthia: "Yes, basically."

You: "And, Gordon, if I understand your position clearly, it's not necessarily that you're against *any* name change—just that you don't think a change to Forest Corner is appropriate and would accomplish any purpose, right?"

Gordon: "Right. I wouldn't agree to the name Forest Corner at all. It sounds cliquish, common."

You: "So basically, you're neither directly opposed to a name change. It's just that Gordon doesn't see a direct need to do so. Maybe, then, we need to discuss the pros and cons of what a name change would do."

By entering the possibly escalating exchange, what you have done is to help both sides see areas of agreement and clarify positions, which in this case were not altogether contradictory. Often, people who are immediately involved in exchanging views don't really listen to each other's position, but instead are planning what they want to say next. Avoiding a break in the relationship may be as simple as helping both sides clarify what they are and are not saying.

Second, when you help two people clarify their positions and see that they *are* in direct disagreement, try to turn the conversation into an exchange of views rather than an all-out attempt to prove the other wrong. You can do this by interrupting the conversation with a summary of both sides and then tack on some comment of yours that will serve to conclude the discussion and turn attention elsewhere: "Well, Marcia, you present a good case for capital punishment right from the Scriptures. And, Martin, you're equally convincing against it. I'm glad I don't have to vote on the issue today. I wish everybody would put as much thought into what the Bible teaches about political issues as you two seem to have done."

If possible, then you can bring up another subject or let the silence that follows serve as a transition in topics. With your wrap-up statement, you have helped leave a good feeling that the discussion has been merely an exchange of views, not an argument.

Finally, if either of the first two attempts doesn't work, suggest that the two people or groups table their discussion before something "more serious" develops: "Come on, let's drop the subject. You two are making me (or us, if before a group) uncomfortable." Such a statement puts them on the spot before others and will usually serve to end the disagreement.

Peacemaking becomes much more difficult, however, when there is a serious break in a relationship. Two people have not only exchanged opposing views on an issue, but their egos have become so wrapped around the episode that the relationship is threatening a break or has already broken. In this case, a peacemaker must make a real commitment. He must be willing to invest time and emotional energy in bringing them together. And willing though a peacemaker may be, he may be afraid to trudge into the middle of the problem for fear of making the break wider, rather than mending it.

But as usual, God never asks us to do something without giving guidelines. Let's look at three peacemaking situations to examine the biblical principles provided in each: Paul's efforts on behalf of Onesimus and Philemon, Jonathan's intervening between David and Saul, and finally, Gamaliel's peacemaking between the Jewish Sanhedrin and the apostles.

The first principle that these conflicts teach is that a peacemaker should treat both parties with respect and show no favoritism. Many a peacemaking effort has been sabotaged when the reconciler treated both parties as if they were a couple of spoiled children arguing over a playground swing. Although the issue may not seem important enough to you, the outsider, to have caused the rift, you will accomplish nothing by implying to those involved that they are being childish, foolish, or stubborn. And the best way to show that you intend to respect them is to insist that they respect each other; don't permit them to make disparaging remarks about the other in your hearing. And be careful that your body language—a raised eyebrow or a knowing grin—doesn't convey favoritism toward the one you're with.

Consider this idea of respect and no favoritism as Gamaliel applied it to the situation recorded in Acts 5:34-42 (Phillips):

> But one man stood up in the assembly, a Pharisee by the name of Gamaliel, a teacher of the Law who was held in great respect by the people, and gave orders for the apostles to be taken outside for a few minutes. Then he addressed the assembly:
>
> "Men of Israel, be very careful of what action you intend to take against these men! Remember that some time ago a man called Theudas made himself conspicuous by claiming to be someone or other, and he had a following of four hundred men. He was killed, all his followers were dispersed, and the movement came to nothing. Then later, in the days of the census, that man Judas from Galilee appeared and enticed many of the people to follow him. But he too died and his whole following melted away. My advice to you now therefore is to let these men alone; leave them to themselves. For if this teaching or movement is merely human it will collapse of its own accord. But if it should be from God you cannot defeat them, you might actually find yourselves to be fighting against God!"
>
> They accepted his advice and called in the apostles. They had them beaten and after commanding them not to speak in the name of Jesus

they let them go. So the apostles went out from the presence of the Sanhedrin full of joy that they had been considered worthy to bear humiliation for the sake of the name. Then day after day in the Temple and in people's houses they continued to teach unceasingly and to proclaim the good news of Jesus Christ.

Notice that Gamaliel did not refer to the apostles as scoundrels or criminals or whatever else was common in that day. Nor did he show up his colleagues by taking the disciples' part in the dispute before the public. Instead, he showed great respect for his colleagues by insisting that the apostles be taken out of the room before he made his remarks in their favor. Their position merited respect and a thoughtful argument, which he gave. Had we not known whose side Gamaliel was on, we'd be hard put to figure it out from his speech. No favoritism, no put downs, just logic and respect.

Jonathan, too, showed this same respect to both his father Saul and his friend David. He refused to let them speak evil of each other in his presence. In fact, he even went one step further. Aware of his father's hatred of David, he spoke well of David in Saul's presence and pleaded with his father to reconsider his plans to murder him (1 Sam. 19:4-7, TLB).

> The next morning as Jonathan and his father were talking together, he spoke well of David and begged him not to be against David.
>
> "He's never done anything to harm you," Jonathan pleaded. "He has always helped you in any way he could. Have you forgotten about the time he risked his life to kill Goliath, and how the Lord brought a great victory to Israel as a result? You were certainly happy about it then. Why should you now murder an innocent man by killing him? There is no reason for it at all!"
>
> Finally Saul agreed, and vowed, "As the Lord lives, he shall not be killed."

And when Jonathan was with David, he defended his father and tried to make David believe the best about him (1 Sam. 20:1-2, TLB). Of course, we know Jonathan was wrong about his father's plans, but the point is that he insisted on helping both men to see the best in each other as long as possible. And through his behavior in the meantime, Jonathan continued to show his love for both without favoritism, still choosing to eat meals at his father's table and to meet with David and assure him of his devotion.

Likewise, Paul, in his letter to Philemon about accepting back his runaway slave Onesimus, showed respect by deferring to Philemon's good judgment. He stated that he had the authority to command Philemon to take the slave back without punishment, but rather he chose to appeal to his kindness (Philem. 8-10, Phillips).

> And although I could rely on my authority in Christ and dare to *order* you to do what I consider right, I am not doing that. No, I am appealing in love, a simple personal appeal from Paul the old man, in prison for Christ Jesus' sake. I am appealing for my child. Yes I have become a father though I have been under lock and key, and the child's name is—Onesimus!

No assertiveness training for Paul; rather respect, deference and appeal.

Where many peacemakers go wrong is in siding with one or the other of the disagreeing parties and then trying to talk the "opposition" over to that side. Frequently, divorcing couples tell us that this is what happens among mutual friendships. Friends begin to take sides and join the conflict instead of remaining neutral and trying to help the couple in trouble.

This mistake is also the reason some peacemakers get "scratches" and bleed during the thorny untangling of the situation. If they have taken sides and listened to disparaging remarks about the other from either one, they're in a tough spot when the two are reconciled. Often, out of sheer embarrassment over what one has said to the mediator, he may drop the peacemaker from his circle when the conflict is resolved. And what's worse: if you've agreed with the derogatory remarks, when the two finally are reconciled, both may turn against you. Of course, remaining neutral and yet helpful to both sides is never easy; that's why peacemaking is a supernatural ability.

Second, work with both sides separately to clarify "facts" and to formulate solutions both can live with. Look for areas of agreement and allow both to save face. The wise Gamaliel had the prisoners dismissed before he discussed the "facts" with the rest of the council and clarified exactly what the apostles preached and what disturbances they caused. In formulating his solution, he drew upon historical facts that made sense to both parties of the dispute.

If the apostles' effort was not of God, the movement would soon dissipate on its own. If it were of God, certainly the Sanhedrin wouldn't want to have set themselves up against God himself. Of course, Peter and the other apostles could embrace the solution, because they knew that they were acting under God's leadership and with his blessing. Likewise, the Sanhedrin could save face by having the apostles beaten and commanding them never to preach again. The disciples only counted the beating an honor and remained free to preach as they saw fit.

The Sanhedrin issued punishment; the disciples were free to preach. Both had a solution they could live with. Both agreed that God should be honored.

In his dealing with Onesimus, Paul followed this same principle. Obviously he had discussed the facts of Onesimus' escape with Onesimus himself. But then he wrote to Philemon also, specifically clarifying that Onesimus had not stolen anything and offering to make payment if he had. He audited the books, so to speak.

Then, after he had the facts straight, he took special care in pointing out their areas of agreement—that they could be no longer slave and master but brothers in Christ (v. 15-16, TLB).

> Perhaps you could think of it this way: that he ran away from you for a little while so that now he can be yours forever, no longer only a slave, but something much better—a beloved brother, especially to me. Now he will mean much more to you too, because he is not only a servant but also your brother in Christ.

Paul also allowed Onesimus to save face even while returning to a master he had wronged by assuring him that he was a "quality" person, one that Paul himself would like to keep around to help him while in prison. He left Onesimus his dignity and Philemon his authority. And he did so, of course, without letting Onesimus forget the true "facts" of the case—that he belonged to Philemon and had done wrong by running away.

Jonathan, too, used this second principle—separate, clarify, and solve. He knew better than to try to get his disputing father and his friend in the same room to discuss the situation when Saul was so angry. Instead, separately, Jonathan talked through the "evidence" that David had been loyal to the king and did not intend to take away Saul's throne.

Then, again separately, Jonathan talked with his friend David, trying to understand his fear of Saul and trying to determine if there really was any plot against David's life.

He did separate; he did clarify the fact; but he couldn't offer an ultimate solution. He settled on the next best thing, a plan for David to escape his father's wrath. Although there was no "success" in bringing both men together in peace, he was wise enough not to try to force them together for his sake. He knew that the pride of both men would be too great to pretend.

When you find yourself mediating between two people in conflict, remember that you must deal with facts, *not* their interpretation of facts. Both parties will accept this clarification of facts from you much easier than from each other. So your wisdom in digging through innuendoes and feelings down to actualities plays a big part in a successful solution.

The third principle of peacemaking: pass on complimentary things each person has said or felt about the other in past times, and express your confidence in their willingness to be reconciled.

Paul goes to great lengths to pass on to Philemon in the letter the good things he has heard about him—his hospitality and his work through the church meeting in his home. Though Paul doesn't say directly where this information came from, obviously much of it had been verified by Onesimus himself in his conversations with Paul. Certainly, the runaway slave had done nothing to contradict the picture and make Paul think less of his master. In other words, Paul wrote to Philemon pointing out the good in his life that Onesimus had verified, and he showed confidence in Philemon's desire to accept Onesimus back like a brother.

And Jonathan, too, rested much of his persuasive arguments about David's loyalty on past goodness his friend had shown.

Specifically, he reminded Saul of David's loyalty in killing Goliath.

Although Jonathan's efforts between Saul and David were unsuccessful, there's great value in helping others recall "the good old times" between themselves and another person. The more memorable those past ties are, the more easily they can form a strong rope pulling them both back together.

Finally, remind both persons in conflict of their common goals and their influence upon others. Gamaliel pointedly asked the Sanhedrin to consider where their punishment of the apostles would lead if indeed the apostles were doing God's will. How could they continue to rail against these preachers if their common goal was to serve God?

Also, Paul in his letter to Philemon continually emphasized the new goal Onesimus had in spreading the gospel—the very same goal his master Philemon had in sharing his house for worship and showing hospitality to others of the faith. And in a very subtle way, Paul, as he signed his letter and mentioned his companions in Rome, reminded Philemon that others would know of his appeal about the former slave and would be influenced by it. "It's a group request," Paul hinted. "We're all counting on you not to let us down."

Third, you remember that Jonathan's success with his father and David held only as long as Saul could agree on their common goal of victory for Israel. Jonathan's efforts at reconciliation failed only when Saul later succumbed to personal jealousy. Because Saul's insanity had caused him to put his own fears and prejudices ahead of the affairs of his kingdom, there was no longer a basis for reconciliation between him and David. With tears of disappointment, Jonathan finally accepted the situation and sent his friend on his way to safety.

When peacemaking efforts failed in the above situation, Jonathan, as a last resort, did what many who don't get along do in the beginning. He let each person go his own way. This will sometimes be unavoidable for present-day peacemakers. All rifts between believers can't be mended. When an unalterable situation develops, we must make the best of it by letting the involved parties go their own ways. But remember that this compromise should be only a last resort, not a substitute for our unwillingness to commit the time and energy to bring others back together.

How to untangle the thorns and weeds of another's relationship? If you're doing the pruning, treat those involved in a dispute with respect and impartiality, insisting that they do the same for each other in your presence. Work with both separately to clarify differences and the "facts" of the situation objectively; then point out the "facts" as you see them. Help them to work out a solution that will meet each person's needs and that will allow both to save their self-respect.

Don't hesitate to help them recall the good times in their past relationship. Share the complimentary comments each has made about the other. Lead them to see what a valuable relationship they are endangering by their present difficulty. Finally, remind them of their common goals and their influence upon others' behavior because of their present conflict.

7

"I keep my mouth shut, but I still feel . . . "

Confronting and Resolving Conflict

In a home where both husband and wife choose each other out of free will and where children are considered a blessing from God, what causes conflict? In a church where God's love is preached, where Christians profess love for their fellowman, where believers have one common goal—to spread the gospel—why is there conflict? In a society that professes belief in God's blessing on hard work and prosperity, why do men and women on the job have trouble working together?

One of the most common breakdowns in human understanding is the mistaken assumption that others share our own viewpoints, expectations, needs, and values. Nothing could be further from the truth. You have only to witness a traffic accident and then to ask the bystanders what they saw to hear several versions of the same facts.

And not only do facts present a problem. Family members and church members have different goals and different methods for reaching those goals. They have shifting value systems that flare up at regular intervals. They compete for recognition, resources, and power.

And although Maslow has identified a hierarchy of needs common to all people, the degree to which those needs are met and the way they are met vary from individual to individual.

Age also contributes to conflict, a problem commonly known as the generation gap. Older people consider it a threat when they've invested twenty-five years of their lives in a cause, charity, or career that a younger person considers a rip-off or waste.

Still other conflicts have to do with the personality, a contentious spirit. The writer of Proverbs had obviously lived with such a spirit when he wrote, "It is better to dwell in the wilderness, than with a contentious and an angry woman" (Prov. 21:19). Due to pent-up anger from childhood, some people become like mine fields. They contain hidden detonators buried into the folds of their personalities, ready to explode at the least provocation.

And finally, conflict seems to come from the very air around us, almost like a germ or a floating cloud of tension that when bumped by a foreign object rains down trouble.

But conflict doesn't have to be one of the negatives of life—at least not after the conflict has been resolved. Actually, a family without conflict, a work place without conflict, a government without conflict, a church without conflict would be an unhealthy organization or institution. Conflict is often the catalyst for improvement. So the next time you see a conflict on the horizon, don't automatically panic and close your eyes on the way through it, hoping to come out of the situation undamaged. Instead, face it with eyes open and a determination to improve the status quo.

The Positives of Conflict

One particular advantage of conflict is that disagreement can lead to better decisions and problem solving. Consider what could have become of the organized church at Jerusalem if the dispute between the Greek and the Hebrew widows had never come to the forefront. Possibly, the apostles would have spent more and more time doing the mundane chores around the church and working to meet individual needs rather than ministering to the larger group. Instead the conflict led the congregation there to organize and elect deacons to carry on the serving ministry of the local congregation. The apostles were then free to pray and preach, allowing the Christian movement to spread all over the world.

A second advantage of conflict is that it spurs intellectual and emotional growth, forcing us to look inward to analyze, justify, strengthen, or discard our own beliefs and values. Look at the change in Peter's behavior after he, the other disciples, and Jesus faced open hostility among the crowds. Before the time of testing and open conflict, Peter had always been the bold one, declaring his loyalty, insisting on his commitment, ready to attack anyone who stood in Jesus' way.

But it was not until Jesus' arrest that Peter was forced to examine that commitment. His three denials in the heat of conflict caused him to weep bitterly for the shallowness of that earlier devotion. The conflict Peter experienced strengthened him. Conflict among present-day followers can have the same soul-searching effect.

Third, conflict is the root of all change. The course of history, including the American Revolution, has turned on the occasion of conflict. Even the spread of the gospel to the Gentiles came as a result of conflict and a frank discussion between Peter and Paul about the audience they preached to and the message they preached.

In present times, we frequently hear and read testimonials that refer to the origins of some great accomplishment as a period of conflict. An overweight person says that he's lost a hundred pounds because of a time of conflict when someone, often a spouse or boss, expressed dissatisfaction with his size. College students who have squandered time and money flunking out of one college and then another testify that a sharp conflict with friend or parent changed their attitude about studying and life's goals. In fact, few people embark on change without some conflict that ignites the fuse of motivation.

Fourth, conflict can make a group more cohesive and can strengthen its cause. Rooting for the underdog is an American phenomenon; watch any disinterested spectator come upon a sporting event and take the side of the team that's struggling from behind. In fact, in countries where Christianity is suppressed, faith flourishes. We know particularly the effect persecution had on the first-century church—growth.

Last, conflict can strengthen individual relationships. For example, Esau and Jacob led lives of duplicity and constant conflict for years, until in their middle age they were afraid even to meet each other again. But once their conflict had been worked out and they were reunited, theirs became a strong bond. They lived a long life together until they both could stand as one by their father's side and bury him in peace (Gen. 35:29).

Likewise, the stronger David's conflict with King Saul became, the closer David and Jonathan grew. At parting, we see them taking an oath of protection for each others' families. First Samuel 20:17 says, "And Jonathan caused David to swear again, because he loved him: for he loved him as he loved his own soul."

Psychologists also tell us that conflict still holds modern-day marriages and families together. Husband and wife who have worked out conflicts and reached agreement about which in-laws to visit on which holidays, how much to spend on vacation, or how often to "ground" a disobedient child, have bonded themselves much closer than newlyweds who've not experienced that first disagreement. And couples who have experienced serious enough conflict to separate from each other for a time and who have then reunited also tell of the stronger bond between them; they have experienced the pain of separation and the investment of time to work out differences.

So, for all these reasons—better decisions and problem solving, intellectual and emotional growth, impetus to necessary change, stronger commitment to a cause, stronger individual relationships— conflict can initiate improvements.

How About Just "Letting Things Ride"?

On the other hand, *unresolved* conflict may lead to increased tension and problems until there is a complete breakdown of communication, cooperation, and commitment.

This was the case in the relationship between Joseph and his brothers. From the very beginning, when Jacob favored Joseph because he was Rachel's son of his old age, the Bible says there was conflict in the household. Joseph's special coat became a tangible symbol of that conflict, and the dreams that Joseph bragged of to his brothers continued to fuel their resentment of him. Finally, their conflict grew to the breaking point, and they entertained the thought of murdering him. Finally, they sold him into slavery.

Frequently conflict destroys a person of little ego strength. Proverbs 18:19 says, "A brother offended is harder to be won than a strong city: and their contentions are like the bars of a castle." The "underdog" or the submissive one in the conflict grows more hostile as the confict wears on until he finally explodes at "the straw that broke the camel's back." Then, of course, the submissive, usually compliant one feels guilty at his "overreaction." He becomes even more depressed and withdrawn about the situation and his lack of self-control.

As a result, unresolved conflict erodes a relationship that may seem smooth on the exterior. But when someone tests its strength, the relationship breaks like brittle candy, never to be restored.

So how do you avoid this danger of letting conflict go unresolved? How do you acknowledge conflict and turn it into a creative catalyst for improvement? Basically, the Bible teaches three ways to deal with conflict: (1) overpowering the opponent and forcing him to accept your solution; (2) withdrawing from the conflict and giving up goals and relationships; (3) and finally, seeking compromise to reach common goals and improve relationships.

The Israelites' release from Egyptian bondage and subsequent conquering of the Promised Land gives many examples of conflict settled simply by God's direction in overpowering the enemy. But of course, overpowering the enemy is not always done by a show of might. Sometimes the submissive and sly manage to overpower and manipulate by their very submission and cleverness, rather than by strength or position. Delilah tricked Samson into revealing the source of his strength (Judg. 16). Laban deceived Jacob into working for him for another seven years to marry his chosen bride (Gen. 29).

But from these examples, we see certainly that "might doesn't make right." In fact, it often makes wrong. The success of winning a conflict and of the majority's suppressing the minority may have little to do with God's will. Of the ten spies sent out to investigate the Promised Land, only two came back to report that they could conquer. The wilderness group went with the majority against God and suffered forty years for their mistake. Although it is *one* way to handle conflict, overpowering the opposition may or may not be God's *best* way in any given situation.

The second method of handling conflict exemplified in the Bible is that of withdrawal or resignation; simply giving up goals, plans, or relationships because of the conflict. Such was the case with Paul and Barnabas (Acts 15:39). The contention between them grew to such a point that they parted company, choosing new partners and new destinations for their missionary activities.

And, on at least one occasion, Jesus himself instructed his disciples to handle the opposition they faced from city to city in the same manner. When you go into a house or city and they refuse to hear you, Jesus said, simply shake the dust from your feet and move on (Matt. 10:14). Sent out as doves among ravening wolves, they were to withdraw rather than fight.

Withdrawal may seem the easiest way to handle conflict for those of us who remember parental training to "be nice" and "don't make a big deal" about things. But easy or not, giving up goals or relationships once cherished feels like defeat.

Seeking compromise is still a third method of handling conflict— compromise that improves relationships and helps us grow. In his conflict with King Nebuchadnezzar, Daniel provides a lesson in creative compromise. Daniel and his three Jewish friends (who had been brought to the king's palace as choice specimens to become personal attendants of the king) had a problem, a real conflict. They didn't want to defile their bodies by eating the king's food. And, of course, supervisor Melzar had been charged with the responsibility to see that they did just that.

But rather than cause a direct clash, Daniel proposed a compromise—the ten-day test in which he and his friends could eat the healthful food to which they were accustomed. And at the end of the ten days, Melzar himself declared them as healthier and wiser than the others. (Dan. 1). God allowed Daniel to resolve the conflict through compromise in order to accomplish the ultimate goal.

Overpowering with force, withdrawal/resignation, or compromise—which method do you chose in working out your own conflicts among friends and family? From time to time, all three.

On occasion, Jesus invited confrontation, such as the time he drove the money changers from the Temple; at other times he walked away from conflict, saying his time had not come.

Whichever method of resolving conflict seems appropriate to your situation, usually you must confront the other person, even if only to discuss the fact that you will agree to disagree and part company. The following guidelines can help you to confront in a manner that will strengthen the relationship and accomplish your goals.

Talking Things Over

Confront Privately on Private Issues

While my husband was in the Navy, stationed in Okinawa, I worked at the Military Education Division. My boss and I got along fine, except for his one bad habit; he liked to swear and tell dirty jokes to his friends who dropped by the office.

At nineteen I hadn't the courage to protest the situation, except to complain to my husband, who was only an enlisted man. But one morning when I reported for work, my boss called me into his office, explaining that my husband had just phoned him and asked him to "clean up his act." I swallowed hard, waiting for the ax to fall. How could Dan have done this to me? We needed my salary!

After a long pause, my boss continued: "I just wanted to apologize; I'll try to watch it when you're around. If I forget, why don't you just get up and close the door between us."

Shocked, I backed out of his office with a meek "thanks." An enlisted seaman third class telling an executive to watch his language? But the more I thought about the situation and how it could have turned out, the more I realized that the result was due to the method of handling the conflict—private confrontation. Had my husband or I confronted him in front of his officer friends, I'm sure the result would have been quite different.

Usually, discussing a conflict in front of an audience either encourages the persons involved to play to the audience or invites a group to take sides, thus enlarging the conflict. When someone raises his voice or otherwise becomes emotionally upset with you in front of onlookers, try to remain calm. Explain that you would like to work out the matter and suggest that you go somewhere private to talk.

Deal with Conflict Promptly

"Let not the sun go down upon your wrath," Paul wrote in Ephesians 4:26. Just as one cancer cell unnoticed and untreated gradually spreads over the entire body, one small untreated conflict can grow until it cuts off communication and cooperation between people. Conflict spreads much like gossip; each time a story is told, the punchline gets bigger. In the same manner, each time a conflict comes to your mind, the cut gets deeper.

Treat the Other Person with Respect

I'm not suggesting a pretentious respect of sugary sarcasm and accommodation. Instead, you should permit the other person to feel like a free agent, not a trapped fly. You convey that respect by thoughtful attention to what he has to say, a tone of voice that is neither patronizing nor antagonistic, word choice that is neither derogatory nor threatening.

When the mob took the woman caught in adultery and held her up to public mockery, Jesus restored her to dignity by putting her accusers on the spot. He challenged those who were without sin to cast the first stone. No matter the conflict, never strip the other person of his dignity and force him to deal with you in a degrading manner.

Listen Until You Experience the Other Side of the Issue

Many people have what writer David Johnson calls a "hit-and-run" approach to conflict; they start a conversation about the conflict, hit the other person with their feelings, and walk away before the other has a chance to respond.[1] Such a method of confrontation tends to build resentment and only prolongs the difficulty—it's only half worked through.

Basically, experiencing the other side makes the same difference in your understanding as feeling sorry for someone with polio and being stricken with the disease yourself. You are in a much more thoughtful position to discuss a problem with someone after you've understood her "facts" and feelings, her goals and her frustrations.

Jesus took this listen-and-experience approach with the people who came to him for help. The rich young ruler who had heard Jesus' message, a message that conflicted with all his prior beliefs, asked Jesus to discuss the inner conflict. First, Jesus listened to the young ruler's recitation of righteous living; *then* he told the young man what was lacking in his life (Luke 18:18-22).

Jesus dealt with Martha's grief at the time of Lazarus' death in the same way. He listened to her feelings about his delay in coming: "Martha said to Jesus, 'Lord, if you had been here, my brother would not have died'" (John 11:21, RSV). We don't have her tone of voice here, but I detect a little blame, a tiny accusation at his delay. But again, Jesus listened to her feelings *before* he explained his intentions to resolve her grief.

Often you can completely calm your opposition by simply inviting him to explain the conflict as he sees it. Then really listen. You may find that you agree with his position. If so, you no longer have a conflict.

State Your Own Needs, Views, Feelings, or Goals

James, in his letter, also told us to ask for what we need: "Yet ye have not, because ye ask not" (Jas. 4:2). Although he was speaking of asking of God, the same truth applies in many cases with our brother. We don't give others a chance to meet our needs. We never even ask.

Psychologists say that's often the case in marriages. Needs are not revealed to the other person. One partner suffers in silence for years, never leveling about his honest feelings. Then one day he or she gives up and walks out of the marriage, using the ultimate resolution to conflict without having first simply asked for what adjustments he or she wanted or needed in the other's behavior.

When people hesitate to level about their true needs, nothing is ever resolved to their complete satisfaction. Being honest means that rather than cloaking feelings and viewpoints in abstract words you try to be concrete. When you say "helpful," "narrow-minded," "liberal," spell out the specifics.

Unless you are willing to be transparent about your needs and feelings as mentioned earlier, conflict-discussions can only be one-sided. Other people can't be mind readers. If you don't level about your views, goals, and frustrations, they can't be dealt with. The other person will go away feeling understood, and you, regretful.

Define Areas of Agreement and Disagreement

The Jerusalem Council and its conflict resolution recorded in Acts 15 gives a good example of an orderly delineation of matters of agreement and disagreement. Evidently at the beginning of the meeting, they got nowhere. Verse 7 mentions that it was after a long discussion that Peter finally took the floor, followed by Paul then Barnabas, then James. After that, the council voted on the compromise decision and sent their delegates on their way to share the result.

What made the difference? Why the long discussion and then the sudden resolution? Peter, Paul and Barnabas, and James focused on agreement: (1) Peter had received a vision from God about Gentile conversions and the Gentiles had been receiving the Holy Spirit. (2) God had blessed Paul and Barnabas' ministry among the Gentiles. (3) Old Testament prophecies had predicted the Gentiles' conversion. So much for agreement. Then the Council moved on to an area of disagreement—whether or not Gentiles should be required to keep Jewish laws. This manner of sorting through the problem and conflict moved them quickly along the path to resolution, stated at the end of the chapter.

I'm sure you've sat in lengthy meetings where people clung to repeating areas of agreement for fear of upsetting anyone. They felt compelled to continue the discussion, however, because the real conflict lurking in the background hadn't been outlined and attacked, much less resolved. Thus, they kept talking in circles, saying nothing new.

Possibly you, too, have met with another person on occasion to discuss a problem, and yet left, feeling that nothing had been accomplished. Instead, you tiptoed around each other's sensitive spots.

It should not be an embarrassment to you to admit having a conflict to settle. Jesus frequently found himself in conflict with the authorities, with those who rejected his message, and even with the disciples when they didn't understand his teachings.

It isn't a sin to have a conflict; the sin originates when you don't settle the conflict in a Christian manner.

Limit Discussion to the Here-and-Now and Keep to One Issue

You remember the Samaritan woman at the well and her attempt to distract Jesus from discussing her present life, her unhappiness, and her immoral relationships. Instead, she tried to sidetrack him with a question about the proper place to worship.

Husbands and wives often play that game; diversions begin with some form of "Well, what about the time you. . . . " All of those trails only lead away from the central conflict that needs resolving.

Guard Against Character Attack

Proverbs 18:14 says: "The spirit of a man will sustain his infirmity; but a wounded spirit who can bear?" You can tell a man that his house needs paint, that his dog has fleas, that his tax instructions are unclear; but you can't tell him that he is dishonest without making him angry.

We sometimes grant the authority to point out character flaws to intimate friends; we give them the freedom to tell us that we are behaving childishly toward our spouse or that we have become sullen and selfish about our possessions. But only with our permission do they take that liberty, and even then the effect is sometimes damaging to the relationship.

Furthermore, we don't appreciate someone's attempt at analyzing our behavior. Only God can examine a person's inner being and assess one's motives. Peter's ability to see through Ananias and

Sapphira's lying about the price of their land and their gift to the church came only by the Holy Spirit's power and direct revelation. Peter alone did not attempt to bring judgment; he left that work to God.

All of us operate from contradictory and inconsistent motivations, motivations that only one with God's wisdom could untangle. Let the Holy Spirit hold the light in the dark corners of others' lives. We need only deal with and resolve the behavior that is out in the open and causing conflict between us.

Finally, be sure when you are dealing with conflict that you describe only another's actions, not his character, motives, or attitudes.

Not:

"It seems that you make this treasury report more difficult to read every month; it seems like you have something to hide."

But:

"I'm still having trouble understanding the treasury report in this format. Would you answer some questions about it for me?"

Make Sure Your Emotions Are Genuine and Appropriate

We've all seen TV sitcoms that depict the crying female as a manipulative schemer. In real life, too, there are those who manipulate by false emotion, be it tears or angry shouts. And much of what we try to pass off as righteous indignation would more realistically fall into the category of sinful stubbornness.

To judge by Jesus' example in dealing with his enemies, few conflicts should move us to anger. A mind and heart full of anger, self-pity, and pride leave little place for the love of God to move in and melt the conflict.

In the 1960s and 1970s, many psychologists preached the benefit of expressing anger, telling parents to permit their children to rant and rave and "let it all out," so as not to damage their psyches. But researcher Carol Tavris writes in her book *Anger: The Misunderstood Emotion* that letting anger out is no more healthy than holding it in. She quotes study after study to show that people who let out their rage do *not* have lower blood pressure or any of the other reactions that are necessarily more healthy for the body. Her conclusions agree with others before her: Find out why you're angry and then choose a more appropriate response.[2]

Again, science and psychology catch up with the Bible. The psalmist gave the same advice centuries ago:

> Stop your anger! Turn off your wrath. Don't fret and worry—it only leads to harm. For the wicked shall be destroyed, but those who trust the Lord shall be given every blessing. Only a little while and the wicked shall disappear. You will look for them in vain. But all who humble themselves before the Lord shall be given every blessing, and shall have wonderful peace (Ps. 37:8-11, TLB).

Analyze your anger, he says. Why be angry and envious when the wicked will perish in the end? Fretting and stewing over the inner conflict only wears you down and accomplishes nothing.

Inappropriate emotion also leaves you defenseless: "A man without self-control is as defenseless as a city with broken-down walls" (Prov. 25:28, TLB).

Instead of lashing out in anger or fretting in depression, the Beatitude gives an alternative: "Blessed are the meek: for they shall inherit the earth" (Matt. 5:5). A meek response comes from a strong, yet controlled person. Meekness applied to conflict is a soothing ointment that heals the hurt without causing more pain or discomfort.

If anything, your emotional response should be one of love. If you want to cry over the conflict, make sure the tears are not manipulative. Instead, let them show love and a desire to mend the break and build the other person up.

Don't Back the Other Person into a Corner

Offer the other person options and opportunities to save face. Even God, when he came to Adam in the garden and asked about disobedience, allowed Adam to hide his nakedness. Ego is a precious thing; stripped of all reasons and/or excuses, people feel exposed and grasp at straws to cover their responsibility and viewpoints. Leave them a fig leaf.

Never Use Your Status

When you attempt to settle a conflict with your status, bitterness develops and hostility continues. Abraham provides a good example of humility in handling his conflict with his nephew Lot. Certainly as head of the family, Abraham could have chosen the most fertile fields for his stock and sent Lot packing; however, rather than pull rank, he allowed Lot first choice and he himself took the leftovers.

Pulling rank is a temptation that few people can resist at the time of conflict. When there's a problem over vacation or time off, who usually gets first choice? We know all too well.

Few of us have learned Jesus' teaching on greatness; consider what suffering he went through without pulling rank and calling on divine power to rescue him from the conflict and rejection he faced on earth.

Don't Be Concerned with Winning or Losing

The way to do that, of course, is to find a way to meet both persons' needs or goals and to avoid placing blame for the difficulty. Does it matter more who spilt the milk or how to clean it up? God promises to call the shots, declare the final winners, and label the losers. And his children should never be losers in anybody's scorebook. Keep in mind the goal of mutual agreement; there's room for everybody in God's winning circle.

That means you should never hesitate to "lose" or apologize. Apologies pack power. Why hesitate and chance a permanent break in a relationship when a few humble words would set the record straight? Undeniably, forgiveness falls within God's plan for his dealing with man and for our dealing with each other.

Some excuses we give for not apologizing sound plausible to us, but not, I imagine, to God.

Excuse #1: "Everybody's allowed to pop off once in a while." True, it's human nature to let self creep through and wreak havoc with relationships from time to time, but that doesn't mean we should give up the struggle!

Excuse #2: "He was wrong, too." That may be true also, but God asks that you try to clear only your conscience, not the other person's. And he did not give instructions to apologize only in the case where we ourselves are at fault. In fact, Matthew 5:23-24 tells us that if we bring our gift to God's altar and remember that our brother has something *against us*, then we should go and be reconciled toward that brother. Notice that the responsibility for apology and reconciliation has nothing to do with who is at fault. If there's a problem between two people, both are responsible to see that it is worked out.

Christian maturity allows no childish games of "You go first." "No, you first." "No, after you." This is one time when "going first" is neither selfish nor rude, but mature and loving.

Excuse #3: "It was such a little thing; she shouldn't be so sensitive."

The wrong always seems small when looking at it from your own perspective. But no matter how insignificant the offense in your estimation, what matters is that the other person's feelings are hurt and something must be done to restore the relationship. As the old saying goes, "Expensive things come in small packages." Likewise, in the same way a toothache can send shivers of agony throughout your whole body, so deep hurts sometimes come in small ways. Let the other person and God be the judge of how small the wrong is.

All three excuses do hold an element of truth or "escape hatch." That's why there are such good rationalizations, that often tempt us to withhold the apology due someone. The solution, however, is not to ignore the uncomfortable barrier between you and the other person, but to learn how to resolve it.

The prodigal son knew the importance of a sincere and well-worded apology. The Bible says that he planned what he wanted to say to his father while he was still a long way from home (Luke 15:18-19). Likewise, we need to give careful thought to *how* we say what we say.

First, make sure that your words show humility. That means that you have to accept total blame for the conflict. As long as you're using such phrases as "I shouldn't have done so and so, but I think that under the circumstances, you can surely see that. . . . " "This really wasn't altogether my fault, you know, because. . . . " "I shouldn't have said that, but you made me so angry when you. . . ." you still have not humbled yourself enough to admit total guilt.

Second, show true sincerity. You may be thinking that if anyone would go to the trouble to apologize, certainly he would be sincere about it. Not always. Some apologizers sound like a criminal on the way to jail who still refuses to express repentance, only sorrow at being caught.

A person may apologize only because it is expedient that the other person think the relationship is mended. One may apologize to keep a job, to please a marriage partner, to regain lost material possessions, or for any number of reasons. If there's doubt in your mind that you mean what you say, chances are that you're insincere about the apology. Save your breath until you have a change of heart.

Third, get specific. Let the person know that you are aware of the pain your thoughtless word or behavior or attitude caused. For example: "I'm sorry that I've been so impatient and snappy lately. When I jumped on you yesterday in front of your family about missing that committee meeting, you must have been embarrassed in front of your kids. That was totally uncalled for and I apologize."

When you are vague about your offense or the pain your words or behavior caused, the other person isn't really sure you understand where you went wrong and how much she suffered. Comments like, "I'm sorry about the mixup or the misunderstanding," ring hollow, because the speaker shows no real understanding of her part in the problem. "If I've hurt you, I'm sorry," implies that actually you are not convinced you have done anything necessary of forgiveness but that you'll be a bighearted, humble person and apologize anyway. The conversation then usually returns to one in which the other must convince you of his position all over again.

Last, make restitution. Receiving an apology without action is like opening a Christmas gift with the batteries not included. If you've destroyed the person's ego with cutting words, offer opinion and evidence to restore his shattered self-confidence. If you've caused others to turn away from that person, do your best to restore their relationship. If you've stolen something—time or possessions—repay. In other words, if you break it, fix it. If you mess it up, clean it up. If you tear it down, build it up again. Only then does the person know you really mean business about restoring the relationship.

And when you're the one to accept an apology, be gracious, remembering the many times God has forgiven you. After any apology—no matter who makes it—there's often an awkwardness in the relationship, a feeling that somehow things may not be the same. There's a time of testing, during which each person carefully tugs at the strings of friendship to see that they're still tied securely.

If possible, arrange to do something together right away—shop, attend a ball game, or simply spend a few more minutes talking about the weather—to put your relationship back on an even keel and make your next meeting more comfortable.

Even with all the above guidelines about handling confrontations, some unresolved conflict is inevitable for the Christian.

But before giving up on finding a resolution, it is important that we decide if we have what Chris Hegarty calls a conflict of needs or a conflict of values.[3] Down through the years, many Christians have claimed conflict of values or principles, when in fact they only felt a conflict of egos.

A conflict of needs can be resolved; a conflict of values can't. For example, let's say you and a neighbor have a conflict over Saturday morning chores. You like to get up early and mow your lawn before the sun gets too hot. Your neighbor stays out late on Friday nights and likes to sleep in on Saturday mornings, without the buzz of a lawnmower outside his window.

In this situation, you have a conflict of needs; he needs undisturbed sleep and you need to mow your lawn before it gets too hot. Conflicts like this can be resolved when two people go about it in a compromising manner. You may both agree on a reasonable hour to start the lawnmower, say 8:00. He gets one more hour of sleep than usual, and you can finish your lawn before ten. Or, you may move your mowing to Friday morning and mow as early as you like.

Or, he may ask you to mow later on Saturday only when he's been out especially late the night before. You compromise; you meet needs.

On the other hand, let's say you and your neighbor have become partners in a part-time money-making hobby of doing odd household carpentry jobs. Some of the jobs are small and paid in cash; your partner, therefore, wants you to ignore reporting those on your income tax for the business partnership. You have a conflict of values. The cheating issue can't be resolved without violating conscience.

Daniel, when he chanced the lion's den because he refused to stop praying to God, faced a conflict of values. Joseph, when refusing to submit to the seduction of Potiphar's wife, faced a conflict of values. Only in such cases does your situation become one without resolution.

In all other matters, God admonishes in Romans 12:18, "If it be possible, as much as lieth in you, live peaceably with all men." The first phrase, "if it be possible" lets you off the hook in case of a conflict of values. The second phrase, "as much as lieth in you," acknowledges that you don't always have control of the circumstances.

But the spirit of the command means that we should be committed to living peaceably and agreeably with our fellowman. To do that, we may have to learn to live with unimportant differences. We may have to modify our behavior and attitudes so as not to offend others. We can try to change others' values so that they agree with us and our Christian principles. And finally, when all else fails, we may have to alter our relationship, so as not to cause constant friction and fret.

Conflict creates a chance to change situations for the better and to grow stronger people in the process. But unresolved conflict festers into a painful break in relationships. So when in conflict, confront.

But remember that in successful confrontations, both persons or groups feel as if their needs have been met and they walk away feeling good about the other person and the resolution.

No losers, only winners of God's peace.

Notes

Unless marked otherwise, Scriptures are quoted from the King James Version of the Bible.

Scriptures marked TLB are taken from *The Living Bible*. Copyright © Tyndale House Publishers, Wheaton, Illinois, 1971. Used by permission.

Scriptures marked RSV are from the Revised Standard Version of the Bible, copyrighted, 1946, 1952, © 1971, 1973.

Scriptures marked Phillips are reprinted with permission of Macmillion Publishing Co., Inc. from J. B. Phillips: *The New Testament in Modern English*, Revised Edition. © J. B. Phillips 1958, 1960, 1972.

Introduction

1. Charley H. Broaded, *Essentials of Management for Supervisors* (New York: Harper and Row, 1947), p. 95.

Chapter 1

1. Harvey L. Ruben, *Competing, Understanding and Winning the Stragetic Games We All Play* (New York: Lippincott and Crowell, 1980), pp. 18,24.
2. Terry Orlick, *Winning Through Cooperation* (Washington D.C.: Acropolis Books, 1978), p. 106.
3. Joe Girard, *How to Sell Yourself* (New York: Simon and Schuster, 1979), p. 24.
4. Robert Weiss, "The Fund of Sociability," *Trans-action*, July-August, 1969.
5. Robert J. McKain, *How to Get to the Top . . . and Stay There* (ANACOM, 1981), p. 27.

Chapter 2

1. Thomas A. Harris, *I'm OK, You're OK* (New York: Harper and Row, 1969).
2. Chris L. Kleinke, *First Impression: The Psychology of Encountering Others* (Englewood, NJ: Prentice-Hall, 1975), pp. 130-132.
3. Adelaide Bry, *Friendship: How to Have a Friend and Be a Friend* (New York: Grosset and Dunlap, 1979), p. 38.
4. Edward T. Hall, *The Hidden Dimension* (New York: Doubleday, 1979), pp. 110,122.

5. Christopher Hegarty with Philip Goldberg, *How to Manage Your Boss* (New York: Rawson-Wade, 1981), p. 181.

6. Dianna Booher, *Making Friends with Yourself and Other Strangers* (New York: Messner, 1982).

7. Robert Bolton, *People Skills* (Englewood Cliffs: Prentice-Hall, 1979), p. 39. See also James Gambrell Robbins and Barbara Schindler Jones, *Effective Communication for Today's Manager* (New York: Lebhar Friedman Books, 1974), p. 53.

8. Art Linkletter, *Yes, You Can!* (New York: Simon and Schuster, 1979), p. 91.

9. Mary Parlee Brown, *Psychology Today*, May, 1979, p. 48.

CHAPTER 3

1. Kleinke, p. 121.

CHAPTER 4

1. Roger A. Golde, *What You Say Is What You Get* (New York: Hawthorn, 1979), p. 109.

CHAPTER 5

1. Sidney Simon, *Negative Criticism* (Niles, IL: Argus Communications, 1978), p. 26.

CHAPTER 7

1. David W. Johnson, *Human Relations and Your Career: A Guide to Interpersonal Skills* (Englewood Cliffs: Prentice-Hall, 1978), p. 282.

2. Carol A. Tavris, *Anger: The Misunderstood Emotion* (New York: Simon and Schuster, 1983), pp. 120-150.

3. Hegarty, p. 293.